Editor
Lorin Klistoff, M.A.

Editor in Chief
Karen J. Goldfluss, M.S. Ed.

Cover Artist
Brenda DiAntonis

Illustrator
Teacher Created Resources

Art Coordinator
Renée Christine Yates

Imaging
Ariyanna Simien
Rosa C. See

Publisher

Mary D. Smith, M.S. Ed.

DAILY W...

Language Skills

GRADE 3

Includes Standards and Benchmarks

- Over 150 daily language warm-ups
- Practice in key language skill areas:
  – Parts of Speech
  – Sentence Structure
  – Vocabulary
  – Mechanics and Usage
- Each warm-up includes a skill review and a writing activity.
- Ideal for test preparation!

GRAMMAR

Author

Mary Rosenberg

Teacher Created Resources, Inc.
6421 Industry Way
Westminster, CA 92683
www.teachercreated.com
ISBN: 978-1-4206-3993-3

© 2009 Teacher Created Resources, Inc.
Reprinted, 2010
Made in U.S.A.

Teacher Created Resources

TABLE OF CONTENTS

Introduction 3

Standards Correlation 4

Daily Warm-Ups 6

Parts of Speech

Nouns. 7

Proper Nouns 9

Singular and Plural Nouns 11

Irregular Singular and Plural Nouns 12

Pronouns 14

Possessive Pronouns 17

Adjectives 20

Comparative Adjectives 23

Irregular Comparative Adjectives 25

Superlative Adjectives 27

Irregular Superlative Adjectives 29

Adverbs 31

Conjunctions 37

Sentence Structure

Complete Sentences 44

Four Types of Sentences 48

Subject of a Sentence 53

Predicate of a Sentence 57

Run-On Sentences 61

Sentence Fragments 63

Vocabulary

Negative Expressions 65

Double Negatives 67

Homonyms 69

Root Words and Suffixes 82

Syllables 88

Spelling Rules 117

Mechanics and Usage

Titles 126

Quotation Marks 128

Colons 133

Ending Punctuation 137

Periods in Abbreviations 143

Commas 147

Apostrophes 151

Dictionary Skills 153

Answer Key 166

INTRODUCTION

In the *Daily Warm-Ups: Language Skills* series, there are over 150 warm-ups that cover a wide range of writing skills: grammar, mechanics, punctuation, and parts of speech. Each warm-up provides a brief overview of a particular skill, an example of using the skill correctly, an activity for the skill, as well as a follow-up writing activity for applying the skill.

In the *Daily Warm-Ups: Language Skills*, the table of contents and the standards correlation chart are useful tools. The table of contents and the standards correlation chart allow you to pinpoint specific skills for each student. The standards correlation chart shows the general skills that a student or child should know at each grade level.

The *Daily Warm-Ups: Language Skills* are ideal for both parents and teachers and are easy to use. For parents, select the skill on which you want to work with your child and preview the page with your child. Be sure to have your child note the topic that is being covered. This will allow your child to access the prior knowledge and information he or she already knows about the skill. Continue to go over the page with your child, so the child will know what to do. When your child has completed the page, take a few minutes to correct the work and address any errors your child made. An easy-to-use answer key starts on page 166.

For the classroom teacher, simply identify the skill page you want to use with the students and photocopy a class set. If several pages are available on a specific skill, you might want to photocopy the pages into individual packets for each student. When presenting the page to your students, start at the top of the page where it notes the topic (skill) that is being covered. By doing this, the students will begin to access the prior knowledge and information they already know about the topic. Then review the first section. This part of the activity page presents information about the topic as well as how the student will be applying the skill. The "Practice" section has the student independently (or with guided practice) apply the skill. The final section—"Write On!"—provides a writing activity that incorporates that page's specific skill.

The skills covered in *Daily Warm-Ups: Language Skills* are skills that are used throughout one's life. Help your child or students master these skills as they will use them throughout the rest of their educational career and life.

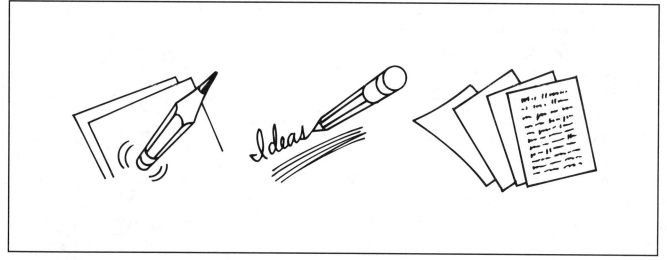

STANDARDS CORRELATION

Each lesson in *Daily Warm-Ups: Language Skills* (Grade 3) meets one or more of the following language arts standards, which are used with permission from McREL (Copyright 2009 McREL, Mid-continent Research for Education and Learning 4601 DTC Boulevard, Suite 500 Denver, CO 80237, Telephone: 303-337-0990, Website: www.mcrel.org/standards-benchmarks)

Standard 1: Uses the general skills and strategies of the writing process

- Drafting and Revising: Uses strategies to draft and revise written work (e.g., elaborates on a central idea; writes with attention to audience, word choice, sentence variation; uses paragraphs to develop separate ideas; produces multiple drafts)

    Sentence variation—pages 61 and 62

Standard 2: Uses the stylistic and rhetorical aspects of writing

- Uses descriptive language that clarifies and enhances ideas (e.g., sensory details)

    Sensory details—pages 20–26, 31–36

- Uses a variety of sentence structures in writing (e.g., uses exclamatory and imperative sentences)

    Exclamatory and imperative sentences—pages 44, 45, 50, 51, 52

    Ask questions—page 49

Standard 3: Uses grammatical and mechanical conventions in written compositions

- Uses pronouns in written compositions (e.g., substitutes pronouns for nouns, uses pronoun agreement)

    Subjects—pages 14, 15, 16

    Possessive—pages 17, 18, 19

- Uses nouns in written compositions (e.g., uses plural and singular naming words, forms regular and irregular plurals of nouns, uses common and proper nouns, uses nouns as subjects)

    Nouns as subjects—pages 7, 8, 46, 48, 53, 54, 55, 56

    Proper nouns—pages 9 and 10

    Singular and plural nouns—page 11

    Irregular singular and plural nouns—pages 12 and 13

- Uses verbs in written compositions (e.g., uses a wide variety of action verbs, past and present verb tenses)

    Action verbs—pages 47, 57, 58, 59, 60

    Subject/verb agreement—page 85

    Past/present—pages 86 and 87

- Uses adjectives in written compositions

    Adjectives—pages 20, 21, 22

    Comparative adjectives—pages 23 and 24

    Irregular comparative adjectives—pages 25 and 26

    Superlative adjectives—pages 27 and 28

    Irregular superlative adjectives—pages 29 and 30

- Uses adverbs in written compositions

    Adverbs—pages 31, 32, 33, 34, 35, 36

STANDARDS CORRELATION

Standard 3: Uses grammatical and mechanical conventions in written compositions *(cont.)*

- Uses coordinating conjunctions in written compositions (e.g., links ideas using connecting words)
  Coordinating conjunctions—pages 37, 38, 39, 40, 41, 42, 43
- Uses negatives in written compositions
  Negatives—pages 65, 66, 67, 68
- Uses conventions of spelling in written compositions (e.g., uses a dictionary and other resources to spell words; uses vowel combinations for correct spelling, compounds, roots, suffixes, prefixes, and syllable construction to spell words)
  Uses a dictionary—pages 162, 163, 164,165
  Compounds—page 90
  Suffixes—pages 82, 83, 84, 85, 86, 87
  Syllables—pages 93–116
  Suffixes/prefixes—pages 88, 89, 91, 92
  Spelling rules—pages 117–125
- Uses conventions of capitalization in written compositions (e.g., titles of people)
  Titles—pages 126 and 127
- Uses conventions of punctuation in written compositions (e.g., uses periods in abbreviations; uses commas in dates and addresses and after greetings and closings in a letter; uses apostrophes in contractions and possessive nouns; uses quotation marks around titles and with direct quotations)
  Apostrophes (contractions)—page 152
  Apostrophes (possessives)—page 151
  Colons (formal letter)—page 135
  Colons (in definitions)—page 136
  Colons (independent clause, list)—pages 133 and 134
  Commas (before conjunction)—page 148
  Commas (dates)—page 150
  Commas (in a letter)—page 135
  Commas (in a list)—page 147
  Commas (intro clause)—page 149
  Periods—pages 44, 45, 51, 52, 137–142
  Periods (abbreviations)—pages 143, 144, 145, 146
  Quotation marks (direct)—pages 128–132

Standard 4: Gathers and uses information for research purposes

- Uses key words, guide words, alphabetical and numerical order, indexes, cross-references, and letters on volumes to find information for research topics
  Alphabetical order—pages 153 and 154
  Guide words—pages 155, 156, 157

Standard 5: Uses the general skills and strategies of the reading process

- Uses word reference materials (e.g., glossary, dictionary, thesaurus) to determine the meaning, pronunciation, and derivations of unknown words
  Dictionary—pages 153, 158, 159, 160, 161
- Understands level-appropriate reading vocabulary (e.g., homophones, multi-meaning words)
  Homonyms—pages 69–81
  Multi-meaning words—pages 160, 161

Name _____   Date _____

Nouns

Nouns name people, places, or things.

Examples: *Person*—president, mom, student
Place—restaurant, park, school
Thing—ball, dish, pencil

PRACTICE

Underline and identify the kind of noun in the subject of each sentence (person, place, or thing).

Example: The fluffy <u>rabbit</u> was in its cage.   _thing_

1. My <u>brother</u> is an amazing swimmer.   *person*

2. The three <u>friends</u> pretend they are cowboys.   *person*

3. The <u>plane</u> flew around and around in circles.   *thing*

4. The <u>cabbages</u> grew to be an enormous size.   *thing*

5. Her <u>teeth</u> were shiny white.   *thing*

6. The <u>restaurant</u> was doing a booming business.   ~~place~~ *place*

7. The salesman sold more <u>cars</u> than anybody else.   *thing*

8. The photographer took all of the wedding <u>pictures</u>.   *thing*

9. <u>Tommy</u> bought a bus ticket.   *person*

10. <u>Milwaukee</u> is a city in Wisconsin.   *place*

Write three nouns for each category.

Person: __*president*__, __*mom*__, __*student*__

Place: __*restaurant*__, __*park*__, __*school*__

Thing: __*ball*__, __*dish*__, __*pencil*__

WRITE ON!

On a separate sheet of paper, write a paragraph using the nine nouns listed above. Share your paragraph with a classmate.

Name _____   Date _____

Nouns

Nouns name people, places, or things.

Examples: *Person*—actor, brother, baby

Place—home, church, hospital

Thing—soda, calculator, stapler

PRACTICE

Read each sentence. Underline the nouns that name people. Circle the nouns that name places. Put a star next to the nouns that name things.

Example: Benson enjoys singing at local carnivals.

1. Eddie was driving the car to Chicago.

2. Mary was working on her medical degree.

3. Their friends collected newspapers for recycling.

4. The alarm was ringing.

5. Dad was in the kitchen fixing dinner.

6. Uncle Teddy was pruning the trees in the backyard.

7. The note cards were made from construction paper.

8. The DVDs were on sale.

9. The fleas were all over the animals.

10. The bed was neatly made.

Name three relatives: __bother__, __room__, __dad__

Name three places (or cities) where the relatives live: __home__, __church__, __hospital__

Name three things the relatives have: __bother__, __sister__, __baby__

WRITE ON!

Use the information about your relatives to write a paragraph on a separate sheet of paper. Trade papers with a classmate. Have the classmate underline all of the nouns used in the paragraph.

Name _____   Date _____

Proper Nouns

Nouns name people, places, or things. A **proper noun** identifies by name the person, place, or thing. Each name in the proper noun begins with a capital letter. Look at the examples below.

	Noun	Proper Noun
Person	teacher	Mrs. Blair
Place	restaurant	Cecil's Fried Chicken
Thing	sneakers	Run Fast Sneakers

PRACTICE

Write a proper noun for each item.

1. park _____ Monbose park _____
2. street _____ Tully St. _____
3. doctor _____ Mr. Collens _____
4. neighbor _____ Thea _____
5. paint _____ red _____

Rewrite each sentence. Change the underlined words to a proper noun.

6. The dog was guarding the yard.
   _____ Doise was guairding the yard. _____

7. The baseball team lost another game.
   _____ The Bestie lost another game _____

8. My neighbor is always barbecuing.
   _____ My Lan is always barbecuing. _____

9. I love to shop at the store.
   _____ I love to shop at Great mall. _____

10. It is a good brand.
    _____ Ceral is a good brand. _____

11. The school has many students.
    _____ Dalmation has many student _____

12. The principal spoke over the loudspeaker.
    _____ Ms Lan spoke over the loud speaker. _____

WRITE ON!

On a separate sheet of paper, write a paragraph on a topic of your choice. Do not use any proper nouns in the story. Underline five nouns used in the paragraph. Rewrite the same paragraph changing the underlined nouns to proper nouns. Which paragraph is easier to understand and more interesting to read?

Proper Nouns

Nouns name people, places, or things. A **proper noun** identifies by name the person, place, or thing. Each name in the proper noun begins with a capital letter.

Examples:

	Noun	Proper Noun
Person	friend	Benjamin
Place	the coast	Morro Bay
Thing	crayons	Super Colors

PRACTICE

Read the paragraph. Rewrite the paragraph replacing the underlined words with proper nouns.

> Victor decided to try flipping a house. Flipping a house means to buy a house, fix it up, and sell it. Victor has many people helping him: <u>a friend</u>, <u>a brother</u>, <u>a business partner</u>, and <u>his cousin</u>. The house is on <u>a street</u> near <u>the park</u>. The house is near <u>an elementary school</u>. Victor hopes <u>a family</u> will buy his house.

Victor decided to try flipping a house. Flipping a house means to buy a house fix it up and sell it. Victor has many people helping him, Benjamin Lan and Richard. The house is on Morro Bay near the Bay. The house was near Sharakawa.

WRITE ON!

Write a paragraph about your family on a separate sheet of paper. Rewrite the paragraph changing the family members' names to their relationship within the family: sister, brother, mom, dad, cousin, etc. Have a friend read both paragraphs and circle the paragraph that is easier to understand and more interesting to read.

Name _____   Date _____

Singular and Plural Nouns

Nouns name people, places, or things. A **singular noun** names one person, one place, or one thing.

   Examples: a pig, one dog, a mother

A **plural noun** names more than one person, more than one place, or more than one thing.

   Examples: the pigs, three dogs, many mothers

Subject-verb agreement means that the subject and the verb "agree" on the number of items.

   Examples: The pig is pink.   NOT   The pig are pink.

               The pigs are pink.   NOT   The pigs is pink.

Read each sentence. Underline the subject's noun. Then write if the subject noun is *singular* or *plural*.

   Example: <u>Noodles</u> come in one color. _____plural_____

   1. The umbrella is red. _____unbrellas_____
   2. The canopies are striped. _____canopies_____
   3. The trophy comes in gold or silver. _____throbies_____
   4. The championship cups come in only bronze. _____cup_____
   5. The necklace was mailed last week. _____necklaces_____
   6. The packages were sent by cargo ship. _____Ships_____
   7. Albert Einstein was a mathematical genius. _____Alberts_____
   8. Herbert, Bubba, and Walt are not mathematical geniuses. _____Walts_____
   9. Morgana doesn't sew. _____Sews_____
   10. The troops don't go camping in bad weather. _____troop_____

Draw a line through the sentences that do not have subject-verb agreement.

   ~~11.~~ She don't know the answer.
   12. He does have the playing card.
   13. We was working hard on the project.
   14. We are best friends.
   ~~15.~~ I is home.

   16. Mom and Dad is traveling by train.
   17. My dog wasn't barking anymore.
   18. The girls is baking cookies.
   19. Mr. McDuff wasn't at the dentist's office.
   20. The cows are black and white.

WRITE ON!

On a separate sheet of paper, write a paragraph on a topic of your choice. Rewrite the paragraph and change the form of the verbs (*is* to *are*, *am* to *is*) in some of the sentences. Have a classmate read the paragraph and circle any sentences that do not have subject-verb agreement. Was your classmate correct?

Name _____ Date _____

Irregular Singular and Plural Nouns

Nouns name people, places, or things. For most nouns that name more than one, an *s* or *es* is added to the end of the noun.

   Examples: pig and pig<u>s</u>   dress and dress<u>es</u>

Some nouns do not change form. The noun can either be **singular** or **plural**. Most of the nouns that do not change form name animals.

   Examples: one deer   two deer
              one moose   three moose
              a sheep   ten sheep

PRACTICE

Read each sentence. Circle the sentences that name more than one animal.

   Example: (I saw many deer.) (The word *many* means more than one deer was seen.)

   1. Ten bison ran out into the road.
   2. Who saw three sheep?
   3. The moose is big and brown.
   4. Do deer travel in herds?
   5. Does the sheep need to be sheared?
   6. Where was the moose?
   7. Does the deer have antlers?
   8. A sheep has curly wool.
   9. Deer live in the woods.
   10. Swine are not fluffy.

Write a sentence for each topic.

   11. Many sheep

   ___I saw many sheep in the WILD!___

   12. A deer

   ___A deer jump over Dindale city.___

   13. Ten moose

   ___Th~~e~~ ~~The~~ Ten moose ran over the motel.___

WRITE ON!

On a separate sheet of paper, write about a time you saw a deer, a sheep, or a moose. Reread the paragraph to make sure each sentence clearly tells whether you are talking about one animal or more than one animal. Clarify any sentences.

Name _____ Date _____

Irregular Singular and Plural Nouns

Nouns name people, places, or things. For most nouns that name more than one, an *s* or *es* is added to the end of the noun.

 Examples: hat and hat<u>s</u>   fox and fox<u>es</u>

Some plural nouns take a different form than their singular partner.

 Examples: <u>child</u> and <u>children</u>   <u>foot</u> and <u>feet</u>

PRACTICE

Write a sentence for each word in each pair of words.

 Example: mouse and mice

  <u>I saw a mouse peeking out through the hole.</u>

  <u>Many mice were hiding in the woodpile.</u>

1. tooth and teeth

   My tooth was about to fallout.
   A person sang My shiny teeth and me.

2. person and people

   Many chair was broken and ha
   People paid money to eat at a
   buffet.

3. ox and oxen

   The ox was angry because his brother kick to
   Oxen was chasing my car.   him, pers

4. goose and geese

   The goose fly by and poop on th chair.
   All geese was fling west.

5. die and dice

   He die after the train crush.
   The dice was on 6 and flip to
   1.

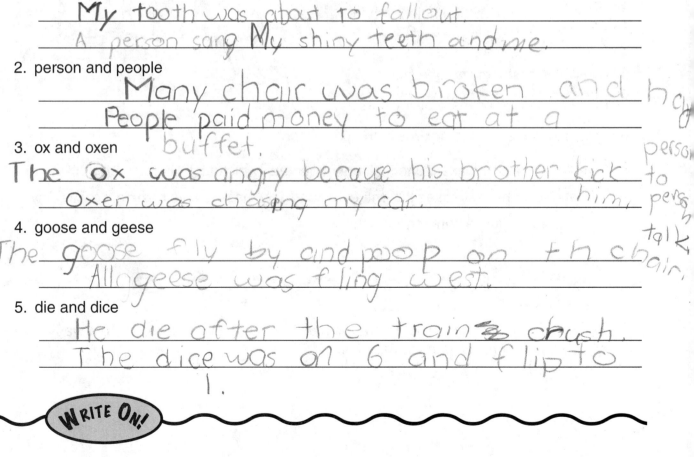

WRITE ON!

On a separate sheet of paper, write a paragraph using at least two different pairs of singular-plural word partners. Exchange papers with a classmate and have the classmate circle the word partners.

Name _____   Date _____

Pronouns

A **pronoun** can take the place of a noun. Singular subject pronouns are as follows: *I, you, he, she, it.* Plural subject nouns are as follows: *we, you, they.*

   Example: <u>Max</u> is a great detective.

   <u>He</u> is a great detective.

The subject pronoun *he* takes the place of *Max.*

PRACTICE

Underline the subject pronoun in each sentence.

1. We are going to the hardware store.

2. You are a great friend!

3. He is fixing the broken shutters.

4. They just moved into the neighborhood.

5. It was lost in the flood.

6. I have two brothers and one sister.

7. She was playing on the monkey bars.

Underline all of the subject pronouns in the paragraph.

   My mom decided to make a photo album of our family pictures. She gathered all of her favorite photos. She really likes the one of my dad and me. He was holding a teeny, tiny minnow. I was holding a humongous fish!

WRITE ON!

On a separate sheet of paper, write a paragraph on a topic of your choice. Have a classmate circle all of the pronouns used in the paragraph.

Name _____   Date _____

Pronouns

A **pronoun** can take the place of a noun. Singular subject pronouns are as follows: *I, you, he, she, it.* Plural subject nouns are as follows: *we, you, they.*

   Examples: <u>Sam</u> has a dog.

              <u>He</u> has a dog.

The subject pronoun *he* replaces the name *Sam*.

PRACTICE

Underline the subject. Write a replacement subject pronoun on the line.

1. Larry is a mechanic. _____

2. The cat was climbing the tree. _____

3. The neighbors threw a big party. _____

4. My friends and I were working in the garden. _____

5. Patsy is the school's librarian. _____

Read the paragraph. Underline the subjects that can be replaced with a pronoun.

   The little duckling was climbing the muddy bank of the pond. When the little duckling reached the green grass, the little duckling began waddling. The little duckling waddled to the boy named Henry. Henry picked up the little duckling and carefully carried the little duckling home.

WRITE ON!

On a separate sheet of paper, write a paragraph on a topic of your choice. Exchange papers with a classmate. Underline all of the subject pronouns used in the paragraph.

Name _____ Date _____

Pronouns

A **pronoun** can take the place of a noun. Singular subject pronouns are as follows: *I, you, he, she, it.* Plural subject nouns are as follows: *we, you, they.*

    Example: <u>Dan and Bert</u> want to be chefs.

             <u>They</u> want to be chefs.

The subject pronoun *they* replaces the names *Dan and Bert.*

PRACTICE

Rewrite each sentence. Replace each subject's noun with an appropriate subject pronoun.

1. Abby and Cash went horseback riding.

    _____

2. Jill ran ten laps around the track.

    _____

3. The ball was flatter than a pancake.

    _____

4. Dorian and I are brothers.

    _____

5. Sid drove the RV to the lake.

    _____

Rewrite each sentence. Replace each subject's pronoun with an appropriate subject noun.

6. I went skydiving last month.

    _____

7. She has the best penmanship!

    _____

8. We packed oranges for the customers.

    _____

9. She earned many merit badges.

    _____

10. It was the best movie!

    _____

WRITE ON!

On a separate sheet of paper, write a paragraph about a favorite movie or television program. Rewrite the same paragraph replacing all of the nouns with pronouns. Circle the paragraph that is easier to read and to understand.

Name _____ Date _____

Possessive Pronouns

A **possessive pronoun** shows ownership. Singular possessive pronouns are as follows: *my, mine, your, yours, his, her, hers, its.* Plural possessive pronouns are as follows: *our, ours, your, yours, their, theirs.*

Example: I have <u>a</u> dog.

It is <u>my</u> dog.

Underline the possessive pronoun(s) in each sentence.

1. Is this your notebook?

2. Her house is always so clean.

3. The dog is wagging its tail.

4. Our garden is full of vegetables.

5. Their boat is blocking our driveway.

6. His skateboard needs new wheels.

7. My name is Emily.

8. The jalopy is mine.

9. The rotting tree is theirs.

10. The suitcase is hers.

Read the paragraph. Underline the possessive pronouns.

   The paramedic responded to the call. He helped the woman get into her chair. Then the paramedic wrapped a cuff around her arm to take her blood pressure. He looked at his watch to keep track of the time. Her blood pressure was fine. The paramedic said, "Your blood pressure is good. It is lower than mine!"

On a separate sheet of paper, write a paragraph about a job you would like to have. Exchange papers with a partner. Have the partner circle all of the possessive pronouns used in the paragraph.

Name _____   Date _____

Possessive Pronouns

A **possessive pronoun** shows ownership. Singular possessive pronouns are as follows: *my, mine, your, yours, his, her, hers, its.* Plural possessive pronouns are as follows: *our, ours, your, yours, their, theirs.*

Example: Why is the <u>Morgans</u>' yard always so untidy?

Why is <u>their</u> yard always so untidy?

The possessive pronoun *their* replaces the proper noun *Morgans.*

Underline the noun in each sentence that can be replaced with a possessive pronoun. Write the possessive pronoun on the line.

Example: The music is <u>Herb's</u>.   <u>his</u>

1. Mr. and Mrs. Hughes' dog jumped over the fence. _____

2. Is this Sally's test? _____

3. The tree's leaves are dropping off. _____

4. The winning raffle ticket is Mabel's. _____

Underline all of the possessive pronouns in the paragraphs below.

Mrs. Macy took her children to the local department store. The family stopped at the boys' department. Zach found a pair of pants in his size. Mom said, "The pants are yours!"

"Yeah! The pants are mine!" cheered Zach.

In the girls' department, Barb found a dress in her size. Her little sister grabbed the dress and said, "I want that dress! That dress is mine!"

Mrs. Macy said, "Go get one in your size."

Barb's little sister came back and said, "Here it is. This dress is my size."

On a separate sheet of paper, write a paragraph about shopping for an article of clothing. Circle all of the possessive pronouns used in the paragraph.

Name _____ Date _____

Possessive Pronouns

A **possessive pronoun** shows ownership. Singular possessive pronouns are as follows: *my, mine, your, yours, his, her, hers, its.* Plural possessive pronouns are as follows: *our, ours, your, yours, their, theirs.*

   Example: <u>The neighbors'</u> house is green.

   <u>Their</u> house is green.

The possessive pronoun *their* replaces the subject's proper noun *The neighbors'.*

Use each possessive pronoun in a sentence.

1. my

_____

2. yours

_____

3. hers

_____

4. mine

_____

5. its

_____

6. our

_____

7. their

_____

8. his

_____

9. her

_____

10. theirs

_____

On a separate sheet of paper, write a paragraph on a topic of your choice. Underline the pronouns. Circle the possessive pronouns.

Name _____   Date _____

Adjectives

An **adjective** describes (modifies) a noun (person, place, or thing).

  Example: The <u>furry</u> dog is barking.

Furry is an adjective. It describes what the dog looks like.

A caret (∧) is used to show where a word or phrase should be inserted (added to) in the story.

                    noisy
  Example: The ∧ children were enjoying the movie.

PRACTICE

Underline the nouns in the paragraph. Use a caret (∧) to add an adjective before each noun used in the story.

   Spot   is   a   dog.   Spot   lives   in   a   house.   Spot   has   a

bowl   and   a   bed.   Spot   has   toys.   His   favorite   is   the   bone.

Rewrite the paragraph neatly on the lines to include your adjectives. Share the paragraph with a classmate. How do the paragraphs compare?

_____

_____

_____

_____

_____

_____

_____

_____

_____

_____

_____

WRITE ON!

On a separate sheet of paper, write a paragraph about a pet you have or would like to have. Be sure to include describing words (adjectives) in your writing.

Name _____ Date _____

DAILY
Warm-Up 15

Adjectives

An **adjective** describes (modifies) a noun (person, place, or thing). An adjective answers the following:

- What kind?   (rubber balls)
- How many?   (seven balls)
- Whose?   (Jack's balls)
- Which?   (that ball)

PRACTICE

Underline the adjective in each sentence. What question does it answer?

   Example: The <u>brick</u> house is on the corner.   <u>What kind?</u>

   1. Pat's donkey kicked the ball. _____

   2. Seven ponies pranced across the field. _____

   3. Ralph's pumpkin was ready to be picked. _____

   4. The tall building almost touched the sky. _____

   5. The pretty girl picked daisies. _____

   6. The cold ice was in the glass. _____

   7. The morning light shone through the window. _____

   8. Ten citizens stood for the salute. _____

   9. That pen doesn't work. _____

   10. This man walked with a cane. _____

Read the paragraph. Underline the nouns. Circle the adjectives.

   Young Ashley went to the circus. She couldn't wait to see all of the exotic animals. Her favorite animals were the gray elephants. Their sparkly costumes shone under the hot lights. Using their flexible trunks, the elephants twirled the fiery batons.

WRITE ON!

On a separate sheet of paper, write a paragraph about a favorite circus animal. Include descriptive adjectives in the paragraph.

Name _____   Date _____

Adjectives

An **adjective** describes (modifies) a noun (person, place, or thing). An adjective can tell the following about a noun: color, size, shape, quantity (number), time, material the item is made from, temperature, age, distance, or purpose.

   Example: The paddleboat slowly traveled the <u>long</u> river.

What kind of river was it? It was a *long* river.

Write a sentence for each kind of adjective.

   Example: color   <u>The *green* leaves fell onto the *dark* ground.</u>

1. color

   _____

2. size

   _____

3. shape

   _____

4. quantity

   _____

5. time

   _____

6. distance

   _____

7. age

   _____

8. purpose

   _____

9. temperature

   _____

10. material

   _____

On a separate sheet of paper, write a paragraph on a topic of your choice. Include adjectives from at least three different categories in the paragraph.

Name _____ Date _____

Comparative Adjectives

Comparative adjectives compare two things. For most comparative adjectives, just add *er* to the end of the word.

Examples: My hamster is small.

My hamster is <u>smaller</u> than your hamster.

In the second sentence, the size of two hamsters is being compared.

For adjectives that end in *y*, change the *y* to an *i* and add *er*.

Examples: My dog is lazy.

My dog is <u>lazier</u> than your dog.

In the second sentence, the two dogs are being compared.

Underline the comparative adjective in each sentence. Identify the two items that are being compared.

Example: The wall is <u>greener</u> than the grass. <u>wall, grass</u>

1. The sofa is squeakier than the chair. _____

2. Marisol's skirt is shorter than Betsy's dress. _____

3. Ivan's beard is rougher than sandpaper. _____

4. French fries are greasier than baked fries. _____

5. The mouse is quieter than the rat. _____

6. Nico eats a healthier diet than his brother. _____

7. Dad's pants are tighter than Uncle Adam's pants. _____

8. The fire burned brighter than the streetlights. _____

9. Knives are sharper than pencils. _____

10. Kevin studied harder for the test than Wayne did. _____

Write a sentence comparing two different animals.

_____

Write a sentence comparing two different books.

_____

On a separate sheet of paper, write a paragraph comparing your favorite food and your least favorite food. Circle the comparative adjectives used in the paragraph.

Name _____   Date _____

Comparative Adjectives

Comparative adjectives compare two things. For most comparative adjectives, just add *er* to the end of the word.

Examples: The passenger train is long.

The passenger train is <u>longer</u> than the cargo train.

Two different kinds of trains are being compared.

For adjectives that end in *y*, change the *y* to an *i* and add *er*.

Examples: The car is grimy.

The car is <u>grimier</u> than the bus.

Two different kinds of vehicles are being compared.

PRACTICE

Use each word to compare two items.

Example: clean   <u>My desk is cleaner than your desk.</u>

1. straight _____

2. messy _____

3. neat _____

4. strong _____

5. sharp _____

6. dusty _____

7. curvy _____

8. smart _____

9. clear _____

10. weak _____

WRITE ON!

On a separate sheet of paper, write a paragraph comparing two different kinds of animals. Exchange papers with a classmate. Have the classmate underline the nouns and circle the comparative adjectives.

Name _____ Date _____

Irregular Comparative Adjectives

Irregular comparative adjectives change form.

For Describing One Item	Comparing Two Items
good	better
bad	worse
little	less
much, many, some	more
far	further

Good is used to describe one book.

 Example: This book is <u>good</u>.

Better is the comparative form for *good*. *Better* is being used to compare two different books.

 Example: This book is <u>better</u> than that book.

Rewrite each sentence using the correct irregular comparative adjective.

1. This gym is gooder than Silver's Gym.

 _____

2. This food tastes worse!

 _____

3. I have littler money in my pocket than in my piggy bank.

 _____

4. I have many cookies than Sara.

 _____

5. He drove far for the reunion than for the wedding.

 _____

6. Who has many puppies than Diego?

 _____

Read the paragraph. Underline the comparative adjectives.

 Sarah and Tracy were working in the garden. Sarah made some rows, but Tracy made more rows. Sarah and Tracy planted vegetable seeds. Tracy planted fewer seeds than Sarah. Sarah and Tracy watered the seeds. Tracy did a better job of watering than Sarah did. Finally, Sarah and Tracy were done in the garden.

On a separate sheet of paper, write a paragraph on a topic of your choice. Change several of the irregular comparative adjectives to the wrong form. Trade papers with a classmate and have the classmate circle the mistakes in the paragraph.

Name _____ Date _____

Irregular Comparative Adjectives

Irregular comparative adjectives change form.

For Describing One Item	Comparing Two Items
good	better
bad	worse
little	less
much, many, some	more
far	further

Examples: This movie was <u>bad</u>.

This movie was <u>worse</u> than the first movie.

The irregular comparative adjective *worse* is being used to compare the two different movies.

Write a sentence for each one of the irregular comparative adjectives.

1. good _____

2. better _____

3. bad _____

4. worse _____

5. little _____

6. less _____

7. much _____

8. more _____

9. far _____

10. further _____

On a separate sheet of paper, write a paragraph about the best (or the worst) day of your life. Remember to include comparative adjectives in the paragraph. Share the paragraph with a classmate. How are your paragraphs alike? How are your paragraphs different?

Name _____ Date _____

Superlative Adjectives

Superlative adjectives are used to compare three or more items. For most adjectives, add *est* to the end of the adjective.

    Examples: I am rich.

              David is rich<u>er</u> than I am. (comparing two items)

              Steve is the rich<u>est</u> of all. (comparing three or more items)

For adjectives that end in *y*, change the *y* to an *i* and add *est*.

    Examples: This cookie is tasty.

              This pie is <u>tastier</u> than the cookie.

              This cake is the <u>tastiest</u> of all.

PRACTICE

Underline the comparative adjective. Write the number of items being compared.

    Example: That was the <u>creepiest</u> movie! <u>three or more</u>

1. Who wore the scariest costume? _____

2. Danielle has the neatest pencil box. _____

3. Chad is hungrier than Chris. _____

4. The chrome is shinier than the glass. _____

5. Which candy is the sweetest? _____

6. Tiny is the biggest elephant! _____

7. Larry's locker is messier than Andy's locker. _____

8. The contest is to find the stinkiest shoes in the school. _____

9. Rachel is the lightest student in the class. _____

10. Teddy is heavier than Samantha. _____

Write a comparative sentence for each set of items.

11. three bowling balls

_____

12. two chairs

_____

WRITE ON!

On a separate sheet of paper, write a paragraph on a topic of your choice. Include at least two superlatives in the writing. Trade papers with a classmate. Underline the superlatives used in the paragraph.

Name _____ Date _____

Superlative Adjectives

Superlative adjectives are used to compare three or more items. For most adjectives, add *est* to the end of the adjective.

Examples: Don is tall.
Dad is tall<u>er</u>.
Mom is tall<u>est</u>.

For adjectives that end in *y*, change the *y* to an *i* and add *est*.

Examples: The baby is sleepy.
The toddler is sleep<u>ier</u>.
The mom is the sleep<u>iest</u>.

PRACTICE

Write a sentence using each comparative adjective.

1. skinniest _____

2. thicker _____

3. smartest _____

4. shortest _____

5. bluest _____

6. bigger _____

7. dirtier _____

8. messier _____

9. blinder _____

10. quietest _____

Read the paragraph. Underline the mistakes.

Antoinette took the harder test of her life! She answered fewest than one hundred questions. She made the tinier of marks next to answers she wasn't sure of. She made a littlest smile next to the answers she was sure were correct.

WRITE ON!

On a separate sheet of paper, write about two happy days in your life. Underline the comparative adjectives used in the writing.

Name _____   Date _____

Irregular Superlative Adjectives

Irregular superlative adjectives compare three or more items. Irregular superlative adjectives change form.

Examples: This soap is <u>good</u>.
This cleaner is <u>better</u>.
This lotion is the <u>best</u>!

Describing One Item	Comparing Two Items	Comparing Three or More Items
good	better	best
bad	worse	worst
little	less	least
much, many, some	more	most
far	further	furthest

PRACTICE

Underline the superlative adjective in each sentence.

1. The airplane traveled the furthest distance.

2. Devin earned the worst grade in the class.

3. Paula had the least number of errors.

4. This was the best conference ever!

Write a sentence using each superlative adjective.

5. best _____

6. worst _____

7. least _____

8. most _____

9. furthest _____

WRITE ON!

On a separate sheet of paper, write about a favorite activity. Try to use at least three irregular superlative adjectives in the writing.

Name _____ Date _____

Irregular Superlative Adjectives

Irregular superlative adjectives compare three or more items. Irregular superlative adjectives change form.

Examples: I ate a <u>little</u> bit of spaghetti.

Cecily ate <u>less</u> than I did.

Marisa ate the <u>least</u> amount of spaghetti of all.

Describing One Item	Comparing Two Items	Comparing Three or More Items
good	better	best
bad	worse	worst
little	less	least
much, many, some	more	most
far	further	furthest

Pick one item from the group and write a sentence using a superlative irregular adjective.

Example: car, train, plane. _____A car travels the best of all._____

1. black, red, purple _____

2. shoes, boots, sandals _____

3. glasses, contacts _____

4. bicycle, moped, scooter _____

5. skateboard, roller skates_____

6. jazz, rock, country _____

7. ocean, pool, bathtub _____

8. apples, oranges, pears _____

9. hamburgers, hot dogs _____

10. puppy, kitten, fish _____

List of three of your favorite things.

_____, _____, _____

WRITE ON!

On a separate sheet of paper, write about the three favorite things. Use at least three irregular superlative adjectives to compare the items.

Name _____   Date _____

Adverbs

Adverbs modify (describe) verbs, adjectives, or other adverbs. Adverbs answer questions. Adverbs tell the following:

• *How* the verb was done	• *Where* it happened
• *When* it happened	• *To what extent* it happened

Example: Joshua eats <u>quickly</u>.

How does Joshua eat? (*quickly*) *Quickly* is an adverb. It gives more information about the verb *eats*.

PRACTICE

Underline the adverb in each sentence.

Example: Nana drove <u>furiously</u> down the road.

1. Frank swung happily on the bars.

2. Allen goes to work daily.

3. The grandfather clock rang loudly.

4. The icemaker rapidly spit out ice.

5. The ceiling fans whirred quietly in the room.

6. The airplane landed safely on the runway.

7. The piglet ate hungrily.

8. The portrait was beautifully painted.

9. The cat purred gently in his sleep.

10. The flowers bloomed brightly in the sun.

Read the paragraph. Underline the adverbs.

   Yvonne dressed nicely for the first day of school. She slowly buttoned her neatly pressed shirt and adjusted her skirt. Her socks were neatly folded over. Yvonne's shoes were carefully shined. Yvonne was finally ready for school.

WRITE ON!

On a separate sheet of paper, write a paragraph describing what it is like to listen to really loud music. Use an adverb to describe each verb used in the paragraph.

Name _____   Date _____

Adverbs

Adverbs modify (describe) verbs, adjectives, or other adverbs. Adverbs answer questions. Adverbs tell the following:

• *How* the verb was done	• *Where* it happened
• *When* it happened	• *To what extent* it happened

PRACTICE

Underline each adverb. Write the question the adverb answers on the line.

Example: The dog jumped <u>happily</u> to its owner.   How

1. The salty popcorn popped noisily in the popcorn maker. _____

2. The lumberjack worked daily in the forest. _____

3. The bus driver finally backed the bus into its parking spot. _____

4. The robot did the weekly laundry. _____

5. The secret compartment was hidden here. _____

6. The genius breezed easily through the difficult problem. _____

7. The superhero had a monthly weigh-in. _____

8. The snake slithered over here. _____

9. The statue tilted dangerously in the storm. _____

10. Her fingers tapped rhythmically on the table. _____

Write a sentence that tells *how* something was done.

_____

Write a sentence that tells *when* something was done.

_____

WRITE ON!

On a separate sheet of paper, write a paragraph on the topic of your choice. Rewrite the paragraph replacing the adverbs with blank spaces. Exchange papers with a classmate and add adverbs to the paragraphs. Compare the two rewritten paragraphs.

Name _____   Date _____

Adverbs

Adverbs modify (describe) verbs, adjectives, or other adverbs. Adverbs answer questions. Adverbs tell the following:

• *How* the verb was done	• *Where* it happened
• *When* it happened	• *To what extent* it happened

PRACTICE

Add an adverb to each sentence.

Example: The snow fell <u>softly</u> to the ground.

1. Step _____ over the uneven path.

2. Grandma drove _____ down the unfamiliar street.

3. With my glasses on, I can see _____.

4. She giggled _____ when called on during the lesson.

5. John _____ made his bed.

6. It was Great-Grandpa's birthday, and he began to dance _____ on the tabletop.

7. The baby cooed _____ when her tummy was tickled.

8. Esther banged _____ on the piano.

9. They rowed the boat _____ down the stream.

10. The tree bent _____ in the gentle breeze.

Write three adverbs for each item.

11. *How* someone might ride a bike: _____, _____, _____

12. *When* someone might arrive for work: _____, _____, _____

13. *Where* someone might park the car: _____, _____, _____

14. *To what extent* something happened: _____, _____, _____

WRITE ON!

On a separate sheet of paper, write a paragraph telling about your ride (or walk) to school. Use an adverb to describe each verb used in the paragraph. Share your paragraph with the rest of the class. (It's okay to exaggerate!)

Name _____   Date _____

Adverbs

Adverbs modify (describe) verbs, adjectives, or other adverbs. Many adverbs end in *ly*.

Examples: quick<u>ly</u>, right<u>ly</u>, snug<u>ly</u>

Adverbs answer questions. Adverbs tell the following:

• *How* the verb was done	• *Where* it happened
• *When* it happened	• *To what extent* it happened

Write a sentence for each topic. Remember to include an adverb.

1. How a pair of shoes might fit:

   _____

2. When the football game will happen:

   _____

3. Where the practice will be held:

   _____

4. How often (to what extent) a person is late:

   _____

5. How a fence is painted:

   _____

6. When the accident occurred:

   _____

7. How often people speed down the street:

   _____

8. Where the flea market is held:

   _____

Read the paragraph. Underline the mistakes. Rewrite the paragraph correctly on a separate sheet of paper.

   Jason careful poured the soda into the cleanly glass. He put a straw into the glass and began noisy slurping the soda. When he was done, Jason banged the glass onto the table. He burped loud and left the kitchen.

On a separate sheet of paper, write a paragraph about trying on something that didn't fit. Maybe the item of clothing was too big or too small. Use as many adverbs as possible to describe trying on the item of clothing.

Name _____   Date _____

Adverbs

Adverbs modify (describe) verbs, adjectives, or other adverbs. Adverbs answer questions. Adverbs tell the following:

• *How* the verb was done	• *Where* it happened
• *When* it happened	• *To what extent* it happened

Many adverbs end in *ly*, but some adverbs do not. Here are some common adverbs that do not end in *ly*.

almost	here	often	still	too	when
around	just	quite	then	twice	yet
down	now	soon	there	very	

PRACTICE

Sort the adverbs from the box above into the different categories.

Adverbs that tell *how* something happened.

_____   _____

_____   _____

Adverbs that tell *when* something happened.

_____   _____

_____   _____

Adverbs that tell *where* something happened.

_____   _____

_____   _____

Adverbs that tell *to what extent* something happened.

_____   _____

_____   _____

WRITE ON!

On a separate sheet of paper, write a paragraph on a topic of your choice. Use at least three of the adverbs that do not end in *ly* in the paragraph. Underline all of the adverbs used in the paragraph.

Name _____   Date _____

Adverbs

Adverbs modify (describe) verbs, adjectives, or other adverbs. Adverbs answer questions. Adverbs tell the following:

• *How* the verb was done	• *Where* it happened
• *When* it happened	• *To what extent* it happened

Many adverbs end in *ly*, but some adverbs do not. Below are some common adverbs that do not end in *ly.* These adverbs tell *when* something happened. (Example: We met <u>yesterday</u>.)

today	tomorrow	yesterday
last year	next month	earlier

PRACTICE

Use each adverb in a sentence.

1. today: _____

2. tomorrow: _____

3. yesterday: _____

4. earlier: _____

5. last year: _____

6. next month: _____

Underline the adverbs in the paragraph.

The new amusement park finally opened! My family went last night. We had a fantastic time! The best ride was the snake ride. It starts off at a high point and drops people through a bunch of s-turns. The ride goes terrifyingly fast. It was the best ride ever!

WRITE ON!

On a separate sheet of paper, write about something that happened in the past. Underline the adverbs that tell *when*. Share the paragraph with the class.

Name _____   Date _____

Conjunctions

Conjunctions are words that join parts of a sentence. There are seven main conjunctions: *for, and, nor, but, or, yet, so.* An easy way to remember these conjunctions is by the acronym FANBOYS.

The conjunction *for* tells the reason why something happened. The conjunction *for* is used instead of *because* or *since.* A comma is used before the word *for.*

Example:

The people were happy to stand up and stretch. They had been sitting for a long time.

The people were happy to stand up and stretch, <u>for</u> they had been sitting for a long time.

Underline the conjunction in each sentence.

1. Doug was digging around in the broken eggs, for he had dropped many shells in the bowl.

2. Marcie's back was tight, for she had been driving the truck for many hours.

3. Billy and Mercy had really bad sunburns, for they had been water-skiing all day.

4. The car was on sale, for it was the end of the month.

5. The mop did not work, for it was falling apart.

Read the paragraph. Underline the conjunctions in the paragraph.

The lion was roaring, for it had not eaten for many hours. The zookeeper forgot to feed him, for he was busy taking care of the sick elephant. That night, the zookeeper remembered he had not fed the lion. He raced back to the zoo. The lion was pacing in the cage, for he was very hungry. The zookeeper gave the lion an extra big helping of burgers.

On a separate sheet of paper, write a paragraph on a topic of your choice. Rewrite the paragraph using the conjunction *for* to combine two of the sentences. Reread both paragraphs. Circle the paragraph that is more interesting to read.

Name _____   Date _____

Conjunctions

Conjunctions are words that join parts of a sentence. There are seven main conjunctions: *for, and, nor, but, or, yet, so*. An easy way to remember these conjunctions is by the acronym FANBOYS.

The conjunction *and* is used when combining two similar ideas.

    Example: Jan used peanut butter to make her sandwich. Jan used jelly to make her sandwich.

        Jan used peanut butter <u>and</u> jelly to make her sandwich.

The conjunction *and* is also used when listing several items. Use a comma before the last *and*.

    Example: Nick washed his socks and his pants and his shirts and his T-shirts.

        Nick washed his socks, pants, shirts, <u>and</u> T-shirts.

Use *and* to combine the sentences with similar ideas.

    Example: The candy bar was delicious. The ice cream was delicious.

        The candy bar <u>and</u> ice cream were delicious.

1. The cars drove down the street. The motorcycles drove down the street.

    _____

2. The music was loud. The music had a good beat.

    _____

3. The house was old. The house was ugly.

    _____

4. Michael dropped the plates. Michael dropped the bowls.

    _____

5. The boys screamed when they saw the rat. The boys screamed when they saw the mouse.

    _____

Read the paragraph. Underline the sentences that could be combined with the conjunction *and*.

    Ella spent the afternoon practicing the piano. She warmed up on the major scales. She warmed up on the minor scales. She played her favorite songs. She worked on her fingering on the difficult songs. Then she was done practicing.

Think about a favorite hobby. On a separate sheet of paper, make a list of things you like about the hobby and how you do the hobby. Use the list to write a paragraph about the hobby. Combine similar ideas using the conjunction *and*.

Name _____   Date _____

Conjunctions

Conjunctions are words that join parts of a sentence. There are seven main conjunctions: *for, and, nor, but, or, yet, so.* An easy way to remember these conjunctions is by the acronym FANBOYS.

The conjunction *nor* is used with *neither. Neither* and *nor* are used in a negative sentence.
   Example: I like <u>neither</u> westerns <u>nor</u> horror films.

Use each pair of words and the conjunction pair *neither* and *nor* to write a sentence.
   Example: sandals, flip-flops
            <u>During cold weather, I wear *neither* sandals *nor* flip-flops</u>.

1. sleeping bag, air mattress

   _____

2. cell phones, walkie-talkies

   _____

3. sticks, bricks

   _____

4. hot air balloon, hang glider

   _____

5. desert, cactus

   _____

Read the paragraph. Underline the conjunction pair, *neither* and *nor*, used in the paragraph.

   Charlene does not like anything. She likes neither hamburgers nor hot dogs. Charlene

does not like mustard. When it is time for dessert, Charlene orders neither ice cream nor

pudding. Charlene is quite the picky eater!

On a separate sheet of paper, write a paragraph on the topic of your choice. Use the conjunction pair, *neither* and *nor,* in a sentence. Underline this sentence in the paragraph.

Name _____   Date _____

Conjunctions

Conjunctions are words that join parts of a sentence. There are seven main conjunctions: *for, and, nor, but, or, yet, so*. An easy way to remember these conjunctions is by the acronym FANBOYS.

Use the conjunction *but* to join two contrasting ideas. Use a comma before the conjunction *but*.

   Example: Thomas wanted to go to the party. His parents would not let him go.

   Thomas wanted to go to the party, <u>but</u> his parents would not let him go.

Use the conjunction *but* to join each pair of contrasting ideas.

1. He was asked to whisper in the library. He was screaming like a maniac.

   _____

2. The car was full of gas. The car would not go.

   _____

3. The telephone was plugged in. The telephone never rang.

   _____

4. The movie was given good reviews. Nobody was in line to see it.

   _____

5. Sally went to the grocery store. She could not remember what was on the list.

   _____

Read the paragraph. Underline the two sentences that express contrasting ideas and could be combined with the conjunction *but*.

   Sophia took a long nap. She threw a temper tantrum when she didn't get her way. Sophia

was sent to her room. She didn't stay in her room. Sophia was having a bad day!

On a separate sheet of paper, write a paragraph on the topic of your choice. Use the conjunction *but* in one of the sentences. Underline the sentence with the conjunction.

Name _____   Date _____

Conjunctions

Conjunctions are words that join parts of a sentence. There are seven main conjunctions: *for, and, nor, but, or, yet, so*. An easy way to remember these conjunctions is by the acronym FANBOYS.

The conjunction *or* suggests an alternative idea or offers a choice.

   Example: Do you want this one <u>or</u> that one?

The conjunction *or* suggests that another possibility can occur due to excluding the other choice.

   Example: You can either study and pass the test <u>or</u> not study and fail the test.

Write a sentence using each pair of words and the conjunction *or*.

   Example: win, lose

      <u>Practice hard to win the game or skip practice and lose the game.</u>

1. early, late

   _____

2. back, front

   _____

3. up, down

   _____

4. pie, cake

   _____

5. anchovies, pepperoni

   _____

Read the paragraph. Underline the sentence that offers a choice. Circle the sentence that shows another possible outcome.

   Tim has decided to go to medical school. He wants to be a dentist or a chiropractor. Tim knows that he has to study hard or he won't get into a good medical school.

On a separate sheet of paper, write a paragraph on the topic of your choice. Include two sentences that use the conjunction *or*. One of the sentences should offer a choice, and the other sentence should suggest another possibility.

Name _____ Date _____

Conjunctions

Conjunctions are words that join parts of a sentence. There are seven main conjunctions: *for, and, nor, but, or, yet, so*. An easy way to remember these conjunctions is by the acronym FANBOYS.

The conjunction *yet* has a variety of different meanings. The conjunction *yet* means *nevertheless, but, in addition to, even, still, eventually, as soon as,* and *now*. Use a comma before the conjunction *yet*.

Example: Bobby was too short to go on the rides, <u>yet</u> he still wanted to go to the amusement park.

Finish each sentence. Use the conjunction *yet*.

Example: Madge was going to wash the dishes, <u>yet her hand was still covered in bandages</u>.

1. He had a lot of money _____.

2. The police car had its red lights flashing _____.

3. The donkey had on a hat _____.

4. Nathan was swinging on the bars _____.

5. The rock star held the microphone _____.

6. The kids were running around the track _____.

7. The pet hotel was full of furry customers _____.

8. Ward and Marianne were on the intercom _____.

9. Senator Grace attended the function _____.

10. The tennis shoes were on sale _____.

On a separate sheet of paper, write a paragraph on the topic of your choice. Use the conjunction *yet* in at least one of the sentences. Share the paragraph with a classmate.

Name _____   Date _____

Conjunctions

Conjunctions are words that join parts of a sentence. There are seven main conjunctions: *for, and, nor, but, or, yet, so.* An easy way to remember these conjunctions is by the acronym FANBOYS.

The conjunction *so* is used to join alternative ideas. *So* shows that the second idea was the result of the first idea. The conjunction *so* shows cause-and-effect. Use a comma before the conjunction *so.*

Example: Marcy did not set her alarm. She was late to school.

Marcy did not set her alarm, <u>so</u> she was late for school.

Use the conjunction *so* to join each pair of sentences.

Example: Frankie went to the store. His pantry is full of food.

Frankie went to the store, <u>so</u> his pantry is full of food.

1. Mariska bought an old house. The house needs a lot of work.

   _____

2. The real estate agent sold the most houses. She was given a large bonus.

   _____

3. Wilma dropped the cookie crumbs on the ground. Many ants came to get the crumbs.

   _____

4. Jason was cold. He made a fire in the fireplace.

   _____

5. Grandpa did not have his hearing aides turned on. He did not hear the doorbell ringing.

   _____

Read the paragraph. Underline the pairs of sentences that can be joined with the conjunction *so.*

   Uncle Ben picked us up to take us to the local water park. The water park was many miles from home. We stopped along the way to get lunch. Once we got to the water park, we had to wait in line to go down the slides. Finally, it was time to go home. Uncle Ben forgot to fill up the gas tank. We ran out of gas.

On a separate sheet of paper, write a paragraph on a topic of your choice. Include at least one sentence using the conjunction *so.* Rewrite the paragraph leaving out the conjunction *so.* Have a classmate read the paragraph and underline the two sentences that could be joined with the conjunction *so.*

Complete Sentences

A **complete sentence** expresses a complete thought. A complete sentence always begins with a capital letter and ends with the correct punctuation mark. There are three kinds of punctuation marks: *period*, *question mark*, and *exclamation point.*

Examples of complete sentences are as follows:

My furry puppy is always chewing on the furniture. (*period*)

Where is the big, red house? (*question mark*)

Our team won the game! (*exclamation point*)

Always check each sentence to make sure it begins with a capital letter and ends with the correct punctuation mark.

Rewrite each sentence so that it begins with a capital letter and ends with the correct punctuation mark.

Example: where do you want to put all of the boxes
           <u>Where do you want to put all of the boxes?</u>

1. have you ever been to an amusement park

   _____

2. it was the best birthday ever

   _____

3. after dinner, we went to the park

   _____

4. how many channels does the television get

   _____

5. i had a horrible nightmare

   _____

On a separate sheet of paper, write a paragraph about a family pet or a pet you would like to have. Proofread the paragraph. Make three lines under the capital letter at the beginning of each sentence. Circle the punctuation mark at the end of each sentence.

Example: <u>M</u>y sister always likes to dress our dog in frilly clothes◯

Count the number of capital letter marks and the number of punctuation circles. The numbers should be the same!

Name _____ Date _____

Complete Sentences

A **complete sentence** expresses a complete thought. A complete sentence always begins with a capital letter and ends with the correct punctuation mark. There are three kinds of ending punctuation marks: *period, question mark,* and *exclamation point.*

- A *period* (.) is used at the end of a <u>declarative</u> (telling sentence) or at the end of a command.
- A *question mark* (?) is used at the end of an <u>interrogative</u> or asking sentence.
- An *exclamation point* (!) is used at the end of an <u>exclamatory</u> sentence. An exclamatory sentence shows great excitement.

PRACTICE

Read each sentence. Decide what kind of sentence it is and what kind of ending punctuation mark is needed.

Example: Dad grew an extra finger   <u>exclamatory</u> <u>!</u>

1. I won the science fair _____ _____

2. Who ate the last delicious cookie _____ _____

3. Go clean that messy bedroom _____ _____

4. Where is Mrs. Richmond _____ _____

5. She actually caught the fly ball _____ _____

Read the paragraph. Identify each kind of sentence and write it above the sentence.

   Mom made a pitcher of lemonade. She put the pitcher on the table. All of a sudden, the cat jumped up on the table. The cat knocked the pitcher of lemonade over! Lemonade went everywhere! What a mess! Mom asked, "Who let the cat in?" My brother and I pointed at each other.

WRITE ON!

On a separate sheet of paper, write a paragraph on a topic of your choice. Be sure to include at least one of each kind of sentence in your paragraph. Rewrite the paragraph leaving off the ending punctuation mark in each sentence. Trade papers with a classmate and add the missing punctuation marks. Compare the two copies of each story. Did the punctuation marks change the meaning of the story or how the story should be read?

Name _____ Date _____

Complete Sentences

A **complete sentence** expresses a complete thought. A complete sentence has both a subject and a predicate.

The *subject* tells whom or what the sentence is about.   The subject can answer the question, "Who or what is this sentence about?"

The *predicate* tells what happens or did happen in the sentence. The predicate is the action part of the sentence. The predicate can answer the questions, "What happened?" or "What did he or she do?"

   Example: Mr. McBride is a dancing machine!

To find the subject, answer the question, "Who is a dancing machine?" The dancing machine is "Mr. McBride."

To find the predicate, answer the question, "What is Mr. McBride?" Mr. McBride "is a dancing machine."

PRACTICE

Underline the subject in each sentence.

   Example: <u>Mr. Stacy</u> is painting the apartment building.

   1. Jason put on his favorite blue shirt.

   2. Mabel practices the drums every afternoon.

   3. Mrs. Cho owns the neighborhood bakery.

   4. Cameron went to the celebration.

   5. Chris likes to play soccer.

Read the paragraph. Underline the subject in each sentence.

   Every summer, Jack goes to camp for three weeks. While at camp, Jack goes swimming and canoeing on the lake. He also does different craft activities. This summer, he made plant hangers and wove potholders. Jack loves going to Camp Fun-in-the-Sun!

WRITE ON!

On a separate sheet of paper, write a paragraph about a favorite activity. Exchange papers with a classmate. Underline the subject in each sentence. Keep in mind that the subject can answer the question, "Who or what is this sentence about?"

Name _____ Date _____

Complete Sentences

A **complete sentence** expresses a complete thought. A complete sentence has both a subject and a predicate.

The *subject* tells whom or what the sentence is about.   The subject can answer the question, "Who or what is this sentence about?"

The *predicate* tells what happens or did happen in the sentence. The predicate is the action part of the sentence. The predicate can answer the questions, "What happened?" or "What did he or she do?"

   Example: Graciela ran after the mailman.

To find the subject answer the question, "Who ran after the mailman?" "Graciela" ran after the mailman.

To find the predicate answer the question, "What did Graciela do?" Graciela "ran after the mailman."

PRACTICE

Underline the predicate in each sentence.

   Example: Marsha <u>was knitting a blanket</u>.

1. Ellen rode her dirt bike over the sand dune.

2. Alex lit the sparkler on the Fourth of July.

3. Evan works as a police officer.

4. Sean is his brother.

5. Rachel runs a day care center.

Read the paragraph. Underline the predicate in each sentence.

   Cat and John went to the movies. They took their little girl with them. Their daughter's

name is Caitlin. The family went to see the latest picture showing at the local theater.

Everyone greatly enjoyed the film.

WRITE ON!

On a separate sheet of paper, write a paragraph about a favorite movie. Exchange papers with a classmate. Underline the predicate in each sentence. Keep in mind that the predicate can answer the questions, "What happened?" or "What did he or she do?"

Name _____   Date _____

Four Types of Sentences

There are **four types of sentences**. The first type is *declarative* or telling sentence. A declarative sentence makes a statement. A declarative sentence always begins with a capital letter and ends with a period.

Examples: I like to drink water on hot days.

On our last vacation, we went to the mountains.

My friend and I went swimming.

Write a declarative sentence about each topic. Remember a declarative sentence always begins with a capital letter and ends with a period.

Example: cats   <u>Cats are furry mammals.</u>

1. birds

_____

2. fish

_____

3. lions

_____

4. turtles

_____

5. starfish

_____

Read the paragraph. Put three lines under the letter that should be capitalized. Make a circle where a period should be. Make a period inside the circle.

last Wednesday, my family and I went to the beach   The waves were calm and gently

came to the shore. While there, my family and I collected many seashells and starfish

at dusk we went back home.

On a separate sheet of paper, write a paragraph about a family trip. Rewrite the paragraph changing some of the capital letters to lowercase letters and leaving out some of the periods. Trade papers with a classmate and see if he or she can find the mistakes!

Name _____ Date _____

Four Types of Sentences

There are **four types of sentences**. The second type is an *interrogative* or questioning sentence. An interrogative sentence asks for information and requires some kind of answer. Interrogative sentences often begin with *who, what, when, where, why,* or *how*. Interrogative sentences always begin with a capital letter and end with a question mark.

Examples: Where is Mom?

Did you see that black car that went speeding by?

Who has answered all of the questions?

Write a question about each topic.

Example: apples How many different kinds of apples are there?

1. potatoes

   _____

2. dessert

   _____

3. juice

   _____

4. watermelon

   _____

5. carrots

   _____

Read the paragraph. Underline the interrogative sentences.

My mom wants to go spelunking. Can you believe that? Do you even know what spelunking is? Spelunking is a fancy name for exploring caves. Also, people who explore caves are called spelunkers. Would you like to be a spelunker?

What questions do you have about spelunking? On a separate sheet of paper, make a list of questions to share with a classmate or with the class. Remember interrogative sentences always begin with a capital letter and end with a question mark.

Four Types of Sentences

There are **four types of sentences**. The third type is an *exclamatory* sentence. An exclamatory sentence shows strong emotion and feelings like surprise, anger, excitement, or fear. When reading this kind of sentence, use your voice or your imagination to convey the strong feelings.

Exclamatory sentences always begin with a capital letter and end with an exclamation point.

   Examples: We won the championships!

            Sheila took first place in the spelling bee!

Rewrite each sentence using a capital letter at the beginning and an exclamation point at the end.

   Example: you should have seen me hit that home run
            You should have seen me hit that home run!

1. they won the game

   _____

2. i crashed my bike into the big tree

   _____

3. i need help

   _____

4. i see a monster in the backyard

   _____

5. the water is so cold

   _____

Read the paragraph. Underline the exclamatory sentences and change the periods to exclamation points.

   We went to the baseball game. The first batter got a walk. The second batter got a hit. The third batter also got a hit. The fourth batter hit a grand slam. The fans stood up and cheered. Our team won the World Series for the first time in fifty years.

On a separate sheet of paper, write a paragraph about an exciting event. Check to make sure that each sentence begins with a capital letter and ends with the appropriate punctuation mark. Make sure to include some exclamatory sentences. Read your paragraph aloud showing strong emotion when needed.

Four Types of Sentences

There are **four types of sentences**. The fourth type is an *imperative* sentence. An imperative is also known as a command sentence. An imperative sentence tells one person or a group of people what to do.

In an imperative sentence the subject, you or all of you, is implied and not expressly used in the given command. An imperative sentence always begins with a capital letter and ends with a period.

Examples: Make your bed.

Go left and then make a right turn.

Rewrite each sentence as a command.

Example: Mark, you need to do your homework.   <u>Do your homework.</u>

1. Sabrina, you need to wash the car.

   _____

2. David, will you rake the leaves?

   _____

3. You all need to be quiet.

   _____

4. Jacob, you need to stop bouncing the ball.

   _____

5. Kenny, will you bake the cookies?

   _____

Read the paragraph. Underline the commands.

   Here are the directions for making pancakes. Take the pancake mix, milk, eggs, and oil and stir them in a bowl. Then you should add a favorite sliced fruit, such as bananas, apples, or blueberries to the pancake batter. Pour small circles of batter onto a hot griddle and cook until golden brown.

Using only imperative sentences, write the steps for doing a specific task, such as making a bed, making a sandwich, or playing a sport. Use a separate sheet of paper.

Name _____   Date _____

Four Types of Sentences

There are **four types of sentences**.

- A *declarative sentence* is also known as a telling sentence. A declarative sentence makes a statement. A declarative sentence begins with a capital letter and ends with a period.

- An *interrogatory sentence* is also known as an asking sentence. An interrogatory sentence asks for information and requires an answer. An interrogatory sentence begins with a capital letter and ends with a question mark.

- An *exclamatory sentence* shows strong emotion, such as anger, surprise, or fear. An exclamatory sentence begins with a capital letter and ends with an exclamation point.

- An *imperative sentence* is also known as a command sentence. A command is an order given to one person or a group of people. A command sentence begins with a capital letter and ends with a period.

PRACTICE

Identify each sentence.

Example: Mr. Carver ate an apple pie.   _declarative_

1. Who is the local judge? _____

2. Don't run red lights. _____

3. I can't find my hundred-dollar bill! _____

4. Mrs. Biko enjoys working in the garden. _____

5. Fold the paper in half. _____

Write an example of each sentence type.

6. declarative: _____

7. exclamatory: _____

8. interrogatory: _____

9. imperative: _____

WRITE ON!

On a separate sheet of paper, write a paragraph on your favorite topic. Use at least one type of each sentence in the paragraph. Rewrite the paragraph leaving off the ending punctuation marks. Have a classmate read the paragraph and add the missing ending punctuation marks.

Name _____ Date _____

Subject of a Sentence

A sentence has two parts, the **subject** and the **predicate**. The subject tells whom or what the sentence is about. The predicate tells what the subject does or did.

The *complete subject* includes all of the words in the subject. The subject answers the question, "Who or what did it?"

    Example: Mr. Knuckles died his hair purple.

Who died his hair? (Mr. Knuckles) "Mr. Knuckles" is the subject of the sentence.

    Example: The large, white stallion jumped over the burning fence.

Who jumped over the burning fence? (the large, white stallion) "The large, white stallion" is the complete subject of the sentence.

Underline the complete subject in each sentence.

    Example: <u>The entire marching band</u> was in the parade.

1. Bobby and Joey rode around and around on the merry-go-round.

2. Edie loves to do arts and crafts.

3. I baked a hundred cupcakes for the carnival.

4. The quiet boy's name is James.

5. Seventeen people rode the subway home from work.

Read the paragraph. Underline the subject in each sentence.

    Boyd and Jessica ride their skateboards to school each day. To be safe, both kids always wear helmets, kneepads, and elbow pads. When crossing streets, Boyd and Jessica carry their skateboards in their hands. The kids put their skateboards carefully in their backpacks when they get to their classrooms.

How do you get to school each day? On a separate sheet of paper, write a paragraph about this topic. Underline the complete subject in each sentence.

    53

Name _____ Date _____

Subject of a Sentence

A sentence has two parts, the **subject** and the **predicate**. The subject tells whom or what the sentence is about. The predicate tells what the subject does or did.

The *complete subject* includes all of the words in the subject. The subject answers the question, "Who or what did it?"

   Example: When it rains, Gina likes to paint portraits.

Who likes to paint portraits? (Gina) "Gina" is the complete subject of the sentence.

   Example: After the hurricane, the little town was completely destroyed.

What was completely destroyed? (the little town) "The little town" is the complete subject of the sentence.

PRACTICE

Underline the complete subject in each sentence.

   Example: <u>The fuzzy teddy bear</u> was sitting on the shelf.

1. The green, leafy tree provides plenty of shade.

2. In the fireplace, the logs were burning brightly.

3. The washer and dryer are always running at the Smith's house.

4. Dad found a hammer and a bucket of nails in the basement.

5. Karen slammed the door shut.

6. The burly firefighter cut a hole in the roof.

7. The patient, painless dentist carefully filled the cavity.

8. Ben likes to think of himself as the king of dirt biking.

9. Jada and Seline play quietly during the baby's naptime.

10. The living room, which is off of the kitchen, is large and messy.

WRITE ON!

On a separate sheet of paper, write a paragraph on a topic of your choice. Underline the complete subject in each sentence. Share your paragraph with a classmate.

Name _____   Date _____

Subject of a Sentence

A sentence has two parts, the **subject** and the **predicate**. The subject tells whom or what the sentence is about. The predicate tells what the subject does or did.

The *complete subject* includes all of the words in the subject. The subject answers the question, "Who or what did it?"

The *simple subject* includes only the main word from the complete subject.

   Example: The luxurious coat is made from purple velour fabric.

What is made from velour fabric? (the luxurious coat) The complete subject is "The luxurious coat." The simple subject is "coat."

   Example: The extremely large football player ran into the goal posts.

Who ran into the goal posts? (the extremely large football player) The complete subject is "The extremely large football player." The simple subject is "player."

Identify the complete subject and the simple subject in each sentence.

   Example: The dream house was demolished.   _The dream house_   _house_

 1. Jerry arrived quickly. _____   _____

 2. The rotten egg smell is from the gas line. _____   _____

 3. The filthy garage needs to be cleaned. _____   _____

 4. The derelict, old factory was sold. _____   _____

 5. The beautiful arched window was broken. _____   _____

 6. The ugly, dead, brown lawn needs water. _____   _____

 7. The old pipes burst during the freeze. _____   _____

 8. The experienced pros can fix anything. _____   _____

 9. The old man hung the picture on the wall. _____   _____

 10. The ringing sound is annoying to listen to. _____   _____

On a separate sheet of paper, write a paragraph about a topic of your choice. Underline the complete subject in each sentence. Circle the simple subject in each sentence.

Name _____   Date _____

Subject of a Sentence

A sentence has two parts, the **subject** and the **predicate**. The subject tells whom or what the sentence is about. The predicate tells what the subject does or did.

The *complete subject* includes all of the words in the subject. The subject answers the question, "Who or what did it?"

The *simple subject* includes only the main word from the complete subject.

   Example: Serena lives in a tiny apartment.

Who lives in a tiny apartment? (Serena) "Serena" is the complete subject. "Serena" is also the simple subject.

   Example: The little old woman lived in a shoe.

Who lived in a shoe? (the little old woman) "The little old woman" is the complete subject. The simple subject is "woman."

Read the underlined part of each sentence. Identify the underlined part as the *complete subject* or *the simple subject.*

   Example: The soft-spoken <u>Mr. Lang</u> wrote a book about space.   simple subject

1. <u>The pig-tailed girl</u> rode the broomstick pony. _____

2. The freckle-faced <u>boy</u> skinned his knee. _____

3. The slim <u>telephone</u> fit in the boy's pocket. _____

4. <u>The small-town bank</u> does a booming business. _____

5. <u>The long-tongued lizard</u> was basking in the sun. _____

6. <u>The honorable judge</u> banged her gavel. _____

7. Is the newly-elected <u>president</u> coming? _____

8. The <u>boys</u> drove the vintage car down the road. _____

9. The dark <u>basement</u> was made of cinder blocks. _____

10. <u>The masked bandit</u> robbed the local store. _____

On a separate sheet of paper, write a story using only simple subjects. Then rewrite the story using complete subjects. Which version of the story is more interesting to read?

Sentence Structure

Name _____ Date _____

Predicate of a Sentence

A sentence has two parts, the **subject** and the **predicate**. The subject tells whom or what the sentence is about. The subject answers the question, "Who or what did something?"

The predicate tells what the subject does or did. The predicate answers the questions, "What did the person do?" or "What happened?" The *complete predicate* includes all of the words in the predicate.

Example: Dad drove the car like a madman.

What did Dad do? (drove the car like a madman) The complete predicate is "drove the car like a madman."

Example: The kids watched the cartoons.

What did the kids do? (watched the cartoons) The complete predicate is "watched the cartoons."

Underline the complete predicate in each sentence.

Example: Mom and Dad <u>went to the new restaurant</u>.

1. Scotty has many friends.

2. Jill and Riley played air hockey.

3. The book was exciting to read.

4. The warm, fuzzy jacket was hanging on the hook.

5. Cassandra jumped over the hoop.

Read the paragraph. Underline the complete predicate in each sentence.

Hercules is a boxer puppy. He has long, skinny legs. Hercules loves to run around the house. He jumps on people. Hercules is a very active puppy!

On a separate sheet of paper, write a paragraph about a favorite animal. Underline the complete predicate in each sentence.

Name _____   Date _____

Predicate of a Sentence

A sentence has two parts, the **subject** and the **predicate**. The subject tells whom or what the sentence is about. The subject answers the question, "Who or what did something?"

The predicate tells what the subject does or did. The predicate answers the questions, "What did the person do?" or "What happened?" The *complete predicate* includes all of the words in the predicate.

   Example: Beth was reading the latest news.

What was Beth doing? (reading the latest news) The complete predicate is "reading the latest news."

   Example: Jamie and John went to the moon.

Where did Jamie and John go? (went to the moon) The complete predicate is "went to the moon."

Add a complete predicate to each sentence.

   Example: Ross <u>was making a hot fudge sundae</u>.

   1. Phil _____

   2. Sue and Mika _____

   3. Kimberly _____

   4. We _____

   5. The cheerleaders and I _____

   6. Ten years ago, my parents _____

   7. The vice president _____

   8. The pudgy bulldog _____

   9. The grumpy cats _____

   10. The jury _____

On a separate sheet of paper, write a paragraph on the topic of your choice. Rewrite the paragraph, but this time leave off the predicate in a couple of the sentences. Trade papers with a classmate and complete the missing sentences. Compare the two finished copies of each story.

Name _____ Date _____

Predicate of a Sentence

A sentence has two parts, the **subject** and the **predicate**. The subject tells whom or what the sentence is about. The subject answers the question, "Who or what did something?"

The predicate tells what the subject does or did. The predicate answers the questions, "What did the person do?" or "What happened?"

The *complete predicate* includes all of the words in the predicate. The *simple predicate* is the main word of the predicate. The main word is a verb or action word. If a helping verb is used, it is also included in the simple predicate. (Helping verbs are words like *is, are, am, was, will,* or *would*.)

    Example: Joanie works hard.

What does Joanie do? (works hard) The complete predicate is "works hard." The simple predicate is "works."

    Example: Jeff is running for office.

What is Jeff doing? (is running for office) The complete predicate is "is running for office." The simple predicate is "is running."

Underline the complete predicate in each sentence. Circle the simple predicate in the sentence.

    Example: Josh is driving the big, red truck.

1. Dorothy is the manager for many rock stars.
2. The grapevines are full of ripe grapes.
3. The senator and her husband listened to the bagpipes.
4. The party was held at the local ice rink.
5. Let's talk about the new job.
6. Tell us about growing lettuce.
7. The desert is full of different kinds of life.
8. Many people attended the performance.
9. The bridge spanned the great river.
10. The computer was making funny noises.

On a separate sheet of paper, write a paragraph on a topic of your choice. Rewrite the paragraph leaving out the simple predicate from each sentence. Exchange papers with a classmate and complete each paragraph.

Name _____ Date _____

Predicate of a Sentence

A sentence has two parts, the **subject** and the **predicate**. The subject tells whom or what the sentence is about. The subject answers the question, "Who or what did something?"

The predicate tells what the subject does or did. The predicate answers the questions, "What did the person do?" or "What happened?" The *complete predicate* includes all of the words in the predicate. The *simple predicate* is the main word of the predicate. The main word is a verb or action word. If a helping verb is used, it is also included in the simple predicate. (Helping verbs are words like *is, are, am, was, will*, or *would*.)

   Example: Mr. Melman has knowledge about the subject.

What does Mr. Melman have? (knowledge about the subject) The complete predicate is "has knowledge about the subject." The simple predicate is "has knowledge."

   Example: The toe shoes hurt her feet.

What did the toe shoes do? (hurt her feet) The complete predicate is "hurt her feet." The simple predicate is "hurt."

Identify the underlined part of each sentence. Write whether it is the *complete predicate* or the *simple predicate*. (Some underlined parts are both complete and simple predicates.)

   Example: People <u>are guaranteed to win</u>.   <u>complete predicate</u>

  1. You cannot <u>win</u> the game. _____

  2. The tape <u>was stuck</u> to his fingers. _____

  3. <u>Raise</u> your hand. _____

  4. The grass <u>grows quickly during the summer</u>. _____

  5. The landlord <u>painted the buildings</u>. _____

  6. The thumbtack <u>was stuck</u> into the bulletin board. _____

  7. The movie <u>was directed</u> by Steven Burger. _____

  8. The food <u>tasted</u> delicious! _____

  9. Your feet <u>stink</u>! _____

 10. We <u>played the trivia game</u>. _____

On a separate sheet of paper, write a paragraph about a topic of your choice. Underline either the complete predicate or simple predicate in each sentence. Have a classmate identify the type of predicate underlined in the paragraph.

Run-on Sentences

Run-on sentences combine more than one thought or idea. The word *and* is used in run-on sentences.

> Example: Jackie filled the piñata with candy <u>and</u> made party hats with streamers <u>and</u> decorated the house with brightly-colored lanterns.

This is a run-on sentence. It has three different thoughts and is very lengthy reading. The same run-on sentence can be rewritten as three separate sentences. The rewritten sentences are much easier to read and understand.

> Example: Jackie filled the piñata with candy. She made party hats with streamers. Finally, Jackie decorated the house with brightly-colored lanterns.

Circle the run-on sentences.

1. Ireland is a small country known for having leprechauns.

2. The train traveled swiftly through the countryside and stopped at the local station and went on to the next town.

3. Zack read the ad in the newspaper and called the number to find out about the lost dog.

4. The explosives went off with a loud bang.

5. Mr. McCann flew the airplane and landed at the nearby airport and refueled the airplane before flying on to his destination.

Read the paragraph. Underline the run-on sentences.

Danny met his friend at the local nursery. Danny and his friend bought many brightly-colored flowers and several bags of potting soil and a couple of different ceramic pots for the backyard. At the register, Danny paid for the items and Danny and his friend loaded the items into the back of the pickup truck and drove home.

On a separate sheet of paper, write a paragraph containing only one run-on sentence. (*Hint:* Use the word *and* in place of the periods.) Rewrite the paragraph replacing the *ands* with periods. Which paragraph is easier to read and understand?

Name _____   Date _____

Run-on Sentences

Run-on sentences combine more than one thought or idea. The word *and* is used in run-on sentences.

Example: Magpie and Cheyenne are the neighborhood pets and everybody loves them and the kids like to play with them.

This is a run-on sentence. It has three different thoughts and is very lengthy reading. The same run-on sentence can be rewritten as three separate sentences. The rewritten sentences are much easier to read and understand.

Example: Magpie and Cheyenne are the neighborhood pets. Everybody loves them. The kids like to play with them.

Rewrite each run-on sentence.

Example: Deborah has red hair and is wearing a pink sweater and is on the horse.
<u>Deborah has red hair. She is wearing a pink sweater. Deborah is on the horse</u>.

1. Bob and Jay are brothers and both of them are firefighters and they each drive red trucks.

   _____

   _____

2. The blankets are in the cedar chest and the linens are in the cupboard and the pillows are on the shelf in the closet.

   _____

   _____

3. Jim is a veterinarian and he takes care of all kinds of animals and he also boards animals overnight.

   _____

   _____

4. The carpenter cut the board in half and placed the board against the wall and he hammered three nails into the board.

   _____

   _____

On a separate sheet of paper, write a paragraph on a topic of your choice. Circle all of the *ands* used in the paragraph. Check the sentences with the *ands* to make sure that they are not run-on sentences.

Name _____   Date _____

Sentence Fragments

A **sentence fragment** is part of a sentence. A sentence fragment <u>does not</u> express a complete thought or idea. A sentence fragment might have a subject or a predicate but not both, or it will not make sense.

Example: A tree.

What is the sentence about? (a tree) "A tree" is the subject. What did the tree do? The sentence does not tell what the tree did. The sentence does not have a predicate. "A tree." is a sentence fragment.

Circle the sentence fragments.

1. A monkey.

2. A monkey swings from tree branch to tree branch.

3. Rebecca returned from the store.

4. The store.

5. Monica and Dave.

6. Monica and Dave went dancing.

7. Marie and Fran cleaned the windows.

8. Cleaned the windows.

9. The button.

10. The button fell off the shirt.

Read the paragraph. Underline the sentence fragments.

   Nicole likes to design clothing. She picked out. She decided to make a dress. The pattern. She carefully cut around the pins. Then Nicole removed the pins and sewed the seams. Was done!

On a separate sheet of paper, write a paragraph on a topic of your choice. Rewrite the paragraph leaving off the subject or the predicate from several of the sentences. Share the rewritten paragraph with a classmate. Have the classmate add the missing element to each sentence fragment.

Name _____   Date _____

Sentence Fragments

A **sentence fragment** is part of a sentence. A sentence fragment <u>does not</u> express a complete thought or idea. A sentence fragment might have a subject or a predicate but not both, or it will not make sense.

Example: Watched the movie.

Who watched the movie? The sentence does not say. The sentence does not have a subject and does not express a complete thought. It is a sentence fragment.

Identify each sentence as a *complete sentence* or a *sentence fragment.*

Example: Taylor quickly.   __sentence fragment__

1. Heather watched television. _____

2. Peter and Ben. _____

3. Mark went to the. _____

4. The mountains. _____

5. The remote control. _____

6. The egg was cracked. _____

7. His skin was very dry. _____

8. She ordered an. _____

9. Interested in getting. _____

10. Billy found. _____

Read the paragraph. Underline the sentence fragments.

   Wesley is a great stunt man. He has appeared. His favorite stunts are jumping off of

horses and tall buildings. Broke many bones. Horse kicked. He hopes to retire soon.

On a separate sheet of paper, write a paragraph on a topic of your choice. Include several sentence fragments in the paragraph. Trade papers with a classmate. Have the classmate circle the sentence fragments.

Name _____ Date _____

Negative Expressions

Some **negative expressions** are *no, not, nobody, none, never, hardly, barely, scarcely,* and *only.* A sentence with a negative word lets the reader know that something is not possible or will not happen.

Example: I do <u>not</u> feel good.

Meaning: The person feels sick.

Example: <u>Hardly</u> anyone brought canned food for the food drive.

Meaning: Just a few people brought canned food for the food drive.

Rewrite each sentence as a negative expression.

Example: I have some money.   <u>I have no money</u>.

1. I am always late for school.

   _____

2. Everybody passed the test.

   _____

3. I can easily hear you.

   _____

4. I have some marbles.

   _____

5. Everyone worked hard in the yard.

   _____

6. Many dogs were at the dog park.

   _____

Read the paragraph. Underline the negative sentences.

   Dennis had had a bad day. Not only did he sleep through his alarm, he also had hardly enough time to eat breakfast. Then his car wouldn't start and he barely made it to work. Dennis hoped he would never have another day like this again.

On a separate sheet of paper, write a paragraph about when you had a bad day. Use negative sentences in the paragraph.

Vocabulary

Name _____ Date _____

Negative Expressions

Some **negative expressions** are *no, not, nobody, none, never, hardly, barely, scarcely,* and *only.* A sentence with a negative word lets the reader know that something is not possible or will not happen.

Example: I have <u>none</u> of them.

This sentence means the person does not have any of a particular item.

PRACTICE

Underline the negative expressions.

Example: There are <u>no</u> apples left.

1. My wife does not want a new roof.

2. The house is not done.

3. She did not build the tree house.

4. I can barely fit into my jeans.

5. Nobody gave me a present.

6. I have never been on a cruise.

7. Hardly anybody is listening.

8. The scratch was barely noticeable.

9. Only a few rides are for children.

10. I have nothing.

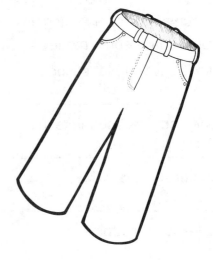

Read the paragraph. Underline the negative words in the sentences.

Ming is a great speed skater. Ming hardly ever falls. He never skates into the walls.

Nobody else skates as well as Ming!

WRITE ON!

On a separate sheet of paper, write a paragraph about a sport you enjoy. Include at least one negative sentence in the paragraph.

Name _____ Date _____

Double Negatives

Negative words are *no, not, nobody, nothing, none, never, hardly, scarcely, barely,* and *only.* A **double negative** means that two negative words were used in the same sentence. A double negative gives the sentence the opposite meaning. The use of double negatives makes a sentence awkward to read. Avoid using double negatives. Look at the two sentences below.

Double negative sentence: This <u>hardly never</u> happens.

Hardly never means that it does happen.

Negative sentence: This <u>hardly ever</u> happens.

Hardly ever means that it rarely happens.

PRACTICE

Underline the double negatives used in each sentence. Write the meaning of the sentence on the line underneath.

Example: <u>Nobody</u> gave me <u>nothing</u>.

<u>Somebody gave me something</u>.

1. I don't want nothing.

_____

2. Only a few gave nothing.

_____

3. Barely no one got away.

_____

4. There was hardly nothing left to eat.

_____

5. Barely nobody came to the party.

_____

WRITE ON!

On a separate sheet of paper, write a paragraph on a topic of your choice. Rewrite the same paragraph using double negatives. Have a classmate read the two paragraphs. Circle the paragraph that is easier to understand.

Name _____ Date _____

Double Negatives

Negative words are *no, not, nobody, nothing, none, never, hardly, scarcely, barely,* and *only.* A **double negative** means that two negative words were used in the same sentence. A double negative gives the sentence the opposite meaning. The use of double negatives makes a sentence awkward to read. Avoid using double negatives.

   Example: We are<u>n't</u> <u>nobody's</u> fool!
       This means the people aren't easily fooled by others.

Rewrite each sentence using one negative.

   Example: I have never not been late.
       <u>I have never been late</u>. OR <u>I have not been late</u>.

   1. I don't have no money.

   _____

   2. She is hardly not speaking to me.

   _____

   3. That answer isn't never correct.

   _____

   4. I can't barely cut through the fabric.

   _____

   5. John doesn't know nobody.

   _____

   6. Caitlin never has none.

   _____

   7. Nobody heard the barely meowing cat.

   _____

   8. She can't hardly wait!

   _____

   9. Mark said that he doesn't need no help.

   _____

   10. Dad can barely get no sleep.

   _____

On a separate sheet of paper, write a paragraph on a topic of your choice. Rewrite the paragraph using double negatives in some of the sentences. Exchange papers with a classmate. Have the classmate underline the sentences that contain double negatives.

Vocabulary

Name _____   Date _____

Homonyms (to, too, two)

Homonyms are words that sound alike but have different meanings and different spellings.

  Examples: *to, too, two*

Below are definitions for *to*:

  A. In a direction
  B. In contact with
  C. For a person

PRACTICE

Read each sentence and underline the word *to*. How is the word *to* being used in the sentence? Write the correct letter of the definition from above on the line.

  Example: Give it <u>to</u> me.   __C__

  1. Who brought the movie to the party? _____

  2. We have a face-to-face meeting scheduled. _____

  3. Jonah went to the store without me. _____

  4. I went to the latest sci-fi film. _____

  5. The dog brought the ball to me. _____

  6. I wrote a letter to my brother. _____

  7. The drill went all the way to the core. _____

  8. We went to Hawaii on a trip. _____

  9. The cans are going to the recycling center. _____

  10. The giant climbed down to the tiny village. _____

WRITE ON!

On a separate sheet of paper, write a paragraph on a topic of your choice. Exchange papers with a classmate. Underline every *to* being used in the paragraph. Have your classmate write the definition's letter above each underlined *to*.

Name _____   Date _____

Homonyms (to, too, two)

Homonyms are words that sound alike but have different meanings and different spellings.

Examples: *to, too, two*

Below are definitions for *too*:

A. also, as well

B. more than enough

C. very extremely

Read each sentence and underline the word *too*. How is the word *too* being used in the sentence? Write the correct letter of the definition from above on the line.

Example: You put <u>too</u> much paint on the brush!   __B__

1. It is too noisy in here. _____

2. He wanted to go to the park, too. _____

3. I ate too many cookies. _____

4. Is this dress too tight? _____

5. You are too late! _____

6. That color is too red for my taste. _____

7. Don't eat too much candy! _____

8. I was too early for school. _____

9. The hole is too deep for the sapling. _____

10. There are too many cooks in the kitchen. _____

Read the paragraph. Write *to* or *too* on each line.

Last month the price of stamps went up again! Now it will cost 53¢ just _____
                                                                                            11

mail a letter. Who knows how much it will cost _____ mail a package. The
                                                              12

price has gone up _____ much! From now on, I will try _____
                        13   14

stay in touch with my friends by e-mail. Hopefully, this won't be _____ hard!
                                                                                        15

On a separate sheet of paper, write a paragraph about how you stay in touch with your friends. Rewrite the paragraph leaving out each *to* or *too*. Have a classmate fill in the missing homonyms.

Name _____   Date _____

Homonyms (to, too, two)

Homonyms are words that sound alike but have different meanings and different spellings.

   Examples: *to, too, two*

Below are definitions for *two*:

   A. *noun*—a cardinal number (1 + 1 = 2)

   B. *adjective or pronoun*—something having two parts or units

PRACTICE

Read each sentence and underline the word *two*. How is the word *two* being used in the sentence? Write *noun* or *adjective*. (*Hint:* Find the noun in each sentence. If *two* is not the noun, then *two* is an adjective.)

   Example: I have lost <u>two</u> teeth. _____adjective_____

   1. I ate two cookies for a snack. _____

   2. The toys came in two separate boxes. _____

   3. Where did those two children come from? _____

   4. Most people have two of each body part. _____

   5. There are two girls on the football team. _____

   6. A bird has two legs. _____

   7. The two of them make a great team! _____

   8. The baby has two pairs of shoes. _____

   9. The two tires are totally flat. _____

  10. Two is a number. _____

Write a sentence for each definition of the word *two*.

  11. noun: _____

  12. adjective or pronoun: _____

WRITE ON!

On a separate sheet of paper, write a paragraph on a topic of your choice. Underline the homonyms (*to, too,* or *two*) used in the paragraph.

Name _____   Date _____   **DAILY**
Warm-Up 66

Homonyms (to, too, two)

Homonyms are words that sound alike but have different meanings and different spellings.
  Examples: *to, too, two*

Which word—*to, too,* or *two*—should be used?

  to: for, going towards   *too*: also, excessive   *two*: number

PRACTICE

Read each sentence. Write the correct homonym (*to, too,* or *two*) on the line.

1. The scooter was given _____ me.

2. I have _____ much junk in my room.

3. He will be _____ years old.

4. Who has _____ cents?

5. Arnie talks _____ much!

6. We went _____ the lake.

7. It rained for many days, _____ .

8. George has _____ left feet.

9. The chair was set next _____ the table.

10. He pressed _____ many buttons!

Read the paragraph. Draw a line through any incorrect homonym. Write the correct homonym above it.

  I have to dogs. Their names are Gracie and Bea. Gracie has a beautiful red coat. Bea is beautiful, two. She is fawn and white. The too dogs are littermate sisters. This means the too of them are from the same litter. (A litter is the puppies that a mother dog has. A mother dog might have one or to litters each year.) The dogs are two funny to watch, but they also give me many headaches, to.

WRITE ON!

On a separate sheet of paper, write a paragraph describing a favorite pet. Rewrite the paragraph, changing the homonyms to the wrong form. Exchange papers with a classmate. Have the classmate draw a line through the wrong homonym and write the correct one above it.

Vocabulary

Name _____   Date _____

Homonyms (to, too, two)

Homonyms are words that sound alike but have different meanings and different spellings.

  Examples: *to, too, two*

Here is one way to figure out which one—*to, too,* or *two*—to use!

- *two*—Try substituting another number, like *three*. If the sentence still sounds fine, then this is the word you need!

  Example: I have <u>two</u> dolls.

  Try substituting *three*: I have <u>three</u> dolls.

- *too*—Try substituting another word, like *also* or *so*.

  Example: I have <u>too</u> many headaches.

    I have <u>so</u> many headaches.

- *to*—Use this one if the other homonyms don't fit!

  Example: I am taking the bus <u>to</u> school.

PRACTICE

Write the correct homonym on the line.

  Example: My dad gave the gift <u>to</u> me.

  1. The TV has _____ many channels to pick from.
  2. Don't lose _____ much weight!
  3. I ate _____ pieces of pizza.
  4. The box lunch was given _____ me.
  5. Let's go _____ the zoo!
  6. The bed is _____ messy _____ sleep in.
  7. Where are the _____ missing cheerleaders?
  8. The desk is next _____ the window.

Write a sentence using each homonym.

  9. to: _____
  10. two: _____
  11. too: _____

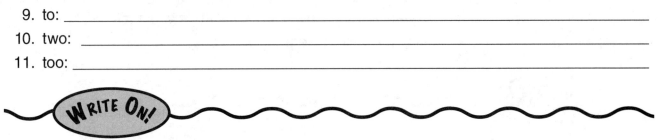

WRITE ON!

On a separate sheet of paper, write a paragraph on the topic of your choice. Underline each homonym (*to, too, two*) that was used in the paragraph. Double-check to make sure the correct homonym was used in the sentence.

Name _____ Date _____

Homonyms (their, there)

Homonyms are words that sound alike but have different meanings and different spellings.

Examples: their, there

Their is a pronoun that shows ownership. Try substituting *our*.

Example: <u>Their</u> house is blue.   <u>Our</u> house is blue.

There is a location. Try substituting *here*.

Example: <u>There</u> they are.   <u>Here</u> they are.

PRACTICE

Underline the homonym (*their* or *there*) used in each sentence. Write *ownership* or *location* on the line.

Example: <u>Their</u> landlord collects the rent each month.   <u>ownership</u>

1. There it is! _____

2. The car is parked over there by the tree. _____

3. Their dog likes to ride in the car. _____

4. Where are their missing coats? _____

5. Their train is late. _____

6. We went there with our friends. _____

7. Have you been there yet? _____

8. Their dorm rooms are near the field. _____

9. What happened to their car? _____

10. Their yard is overgrowing with beautiful plants. _____

Read the paragraph and underline the homophones *(their* or *there)* used in the paragraph.

   Steve and I went to camp. While we were there, we learned to do many new things. The camp leader taught us how to canoe, build a fire, and make a shelter. While there, we also met three brothers. Their names were Billy, Bobby, and Benny. This was their first time at camp, too. Steve and I were glad that we went there this summer.

WRITE ON!

On a separate sheet of paper, write a paragraph about what you would like to do if you were able to go to camp. Underline the homonyms (*their* or *there*) used in the paragraph. Rewrite the paragraph changing the homonym *their* to *our* and *there* to *here*. Does the paragraph still make sense? If not, double-check to make sure you used the correct homonym.

Vocabulary

Name _____ Date _____

Homonyms (their, there, they're)

Homonyms are words that sound alike but have different meanings and different spellings.

   Examples: *their, there, they're*

Their is a pronoun that shows ownership. Try substituting *our*.

   Example: <u>Their</u> house is blue.   <u>Our</u> house is blue.

There is a location. Try substituting *here.*

   Example: <u>There</u> they are.   <u>Here</u> they are.

They're is a contraction of *they are*. Try substituting *they are.*

   Example: <u>They're</u> always late.   <u>They are</u> always late.

Write the correct homonym on the line.

   Example: The tissue is over <u>there</u>.

   1. _____ dessert was put on the table.

   2. _____ donating a million dollars to the hospital.

   3. We went to _____ house for dinner.

   4. Have you ever been _____ before?

   5. The dogs are in _____ doghouse.

   6. They mailed out _____ holiday cards in August!

   7. In September, _____ going on a cruise.

   8. _____ latest invention is sure to be a hit!

   9. They parked _____ RV in front of the house.

  10. The driveway was damaged by _____ carelessness.

Write a sentence using each homonym.

  11. Their: _____

  12. There: _____

  13. They're: _____

On a separate sheet of paper, write a paragraph describing your neighborhood. Underline the homonyms used in the paragraph. Double-check to make sure you used the correct homonym in each sentence.

Name _____   Date _____

Homonyms (their, there, they're)

Homonyms are words that sound alike but have different meanings and different spellings.

Examples: *their, there, they're*

Their is a pronoun that shows ownership. Try substituting *our*.

Example: <u>Their</u> house is blue.   <u>Our</u> house is blue.

There is a location. Try substituting *here*.

Example: <u>There</u> they are.   <u>Here</u> they are.

They're is a contraction of *they are*. Try substituting *they are.*

Example: <u>They're</u> always late.   <u>They are</u> always late.

Write the correct homonym on the line.

Example: <u>They're</u> watching <u>their</u> favorite program.

1. _____ in the same class.

2. The Wilsons found _____ lost cat.

3. _____ she is!

4. Where are _____ shoes and socks?

5. The market is over _____.

6. We went _____ today.

7. The boys played _____ drums like a bunch of maniacs.

8. _____ holding a big reunion _____ next week.

9. I found _____ lucky charm.

10. Do you like _____ drawings?

Read the paragraph. Write the correct homonym on each line.

_____ boat is painted bright blue. Bright blue is _____ favorite color. The boat is over _____ by the canoe. _____ lucky to have _____ own boat. _____ going to take _____ boat out today. If we get over _____, we can go, too!

On a separate sheet of paper, write a paragraph on a topic of your choice. Try to use all three homonyms (*their, there, they're*) in the paragraph. Underline the homonyms.

Homonyms (our, are)

Homonyms are words that sound alike but have different meanings and different spellings.

   Example: *our, are*

Our is a possessive pronoun. It shows ownership. When in doubt, try substituting *my* for *our*.

   Example: <u>Our</u> house is three blocks away.

   <u>My</u> house is three blocks away.

Are is a helping verb. Use this one if *our* (*my*) does not make sense.

   Example: We <u>are</u> going to the play.

Write the correct homonym (*our, are*) on the line.

   Example: Who wants to clean <u>our</u> house?

1. _____ town is having a celebration.

2. We _____ lucky to be here.

3. Where is _____ house key?

4. We can move _____ computer to the office.

5. The glasses _____ shiny and clean.

6. We put _____ toys away neatly.

7. The trophies _____ all on the shelf.

8. We _____ wearing matching outfits.

9. When _____ we going to New York City?

10. What happened to _____ garage?

Read the paragraph. Write the correct homonym (*our* or *are*) on the line.

   _____ classes decided to make a float for _____ town's

parade. We _____ going to use different-colored flowers, streamers, and tissue

paper. _____ families will help us put the decorations on _____

float. When we _____ done, _____ float will be the best-looking

one in the parade!

Have you ever been to a parade? What kinds of floats did you see? On a separate sheet of paper, describe how a float was decorated. Underline the homonyms (*are, our*) used in the paragraph. Double-check to make sure the correct homonym was used in each sentence.

Name _____   Date _____

Homonyms (are, hour, our)

Homonyms are words that sound alike but have different meanings and different spellings.
   Example: *are, hour, our*

Our is a possessive pronoun. It shows ownership. When in doubt, try substituting *my* for *our.*
   Example: <u>Our</u> meal was delicious!
            <u>My</u> meal was delicious!

Hour is used when telling time. When in doubt, try substituting *minute* for *hour.*
   Example: The movie lasted three <u>hours</u>.
             The movie lasted three <u>minutes</u>.

Are is a helping verb. Use this one if *our* (*my*) or *hour* (*minute*) does not make sense.
   Example: They <u>are</u> visiting relatives in another city.

PRACTICE

Write the correct homonym (*are, hour, our*) on the line.
   Example: We go to recess in one <u>hour</u>.

   1. It says to bake the brownies for an _____.
   2. Who knows when _____ science project is due?
   3. _____ they coming to the awards assembly?
   4. The principal said that we _____ excellent students.
   5. _____ relatives come from all around the world.
   6. The _____ is almost up.
   7. We all brought _____ pennies for the fundraiser.
   8. We _____ always last for lunch.

Read the paragraph. Draw a line through any incorrect homonym. Write the correct homonym above it.

   Next month, are class will go on a field trip. We hour going to the local museum. We will

arrive the very our the museum opens. The museum is the first one to exhibit *Cowboys of*

the Wild West. This is a very famous exhibit, and hour class is excited to view it. Many of

are parents will be going with us. They said that they wanted to be hour chaperones, but we

know the parents our also excited to see the cowboy exhibit.

WRITE ON!

On a separate sheet of paper, write a paragraph about a favorite field trip. Underline the
homonyms (*are, hour, our*) used in the paragraph. Double-check to make sure the correct
homonym was used in the sentence. Share the paragraph with the class.

Name _____ Date _____

Homonyms (know, no)

Homonyms are words that sound alike but have different meanings and different spellings.

Example: *know, no*

No is an adverb. It means "not" or "not able to do something." When in doubt, try substituting *yes* for *no*.

Example: I said, "No!"

I said, "Yes!"

Know is a verb. It means to be aware of or to have knowledge of something.

Example: I know the answer!

Write the correct homonym (*know, no*) on the line.

1. I _____ the answer to the question.
2. Do you _____ the way to San Jose?
3. Did Dad say _____?
4. I have _____ marbles.
5. He has _____ award ribbons, but he has three trophies.
6. If you study hard, you will _____ the answers for the test.
7. If you don't study hard, you will not _____ the answers for the test.
8. She has _____ lunch money.
9. Do you _____ how to make biscotti?
10. _____ is the opposite of *yes*.

Read the paragraph. Write the correct homonym (*know, no*) on the line.

Do you _____ if Sandy is coming to the sleepover? I asked her but she
            11
said that her parents had not said yes or _____, yet. I hope she gets to
                                   12
come, because I _____ she will have a great time! We are going to eat lots of
             13
popcorn, paint our nails, and, who _____, we might even do our hair! I hope
                           14
her parents say yes and not _____!
                        15

WRITE ON!

Have you ever had a sleepover or been to a sleepover? What would you tell someone who has never been to a sleepover before? On a separate sheet of paper, write a paragraph about this subject. Double-check the paragraph to make sure the correct homonym (*know, no*) was used in the sentence.

Name _____   Date _____

Homonyms (your, you're)

Homonyms are words that sound alike but have different meanings and different spellings.

Example: *your, you're*

Your is a possessive pronoun. When in doubt try substituting *my* for *your.*

Example: This is your pencil.

This is my pencil.

You're is a contraction of *you are.* When in doubt, break the contraction apart and substitute *you are* for *you're.*

Example: You're my friend.

You are my friend.

Write the correct homonym (*your, you're*) on the line.

Example: You're the best!

1. Where is _____ homework?

2. _____ late again!

3. _____ in my beanbag chair.

4. _____ pillow is so comfortable.

5. Make sure you knock on _____ brother's door before going in.

6. _____ pants are too big!

7. Please turn off _____ cell phone.

8. Keep _____ fingers out of the cookie dough.

Read the paragraph. Draw a line through the incorrect homonym. Write the correct homonym (*your, you're*) above the line.

I pick you and Drew to be on my team. Your both the best players in the class. With you're

help, I know we can win the play-offs at lunchtime. Here is the plan. You will kick the ball

hard and then get on base. Then Drew will kick next and she will kick the ball hard, too.

Once your both on base, I know you will be able to make it home and score the winning runs!

On a separate sheet of paper, write a paragraph about a favorite lunchtime sport or game. How is the game played? What is your favorite thing about the game? Include some homonyms.

Name _____   Date _____

Homonyms (its, it's)

Homonyms are words that sound alike but have different meanings and different spellings.

   Examples: *its, it's*

Its is a possessive pronoun. When in doubt, try substituting *his* or *her* for *its.*

   Example: The dog is wagging <u>its</u> tail.

   The dog is wagging <u>his</u> tail.

   The dog is wagging <u>her</u> tail.

It's is a contraction of *it is*. When in doubt, break apart the contraction and use *it is* in place of *it's.*

   Example: <u>It's</u> hot in here.

   <u>It is</u> hot in here.

Write the correct homonym (*its, it's*) on the line.

   Example: <u>It's</u> all mine!

   1. The cat wags _____ tail when it is happy.

   2. _____ time for the game show to start.

   3. _____ a good thing you're here!

   4. We worked hard to fill the container with _____ contents.

   5. _____ a very busy time of year.

   6. The pig ate _____ fill of the truffles.

   7. _____ going to be another hot day!

   8. Don't ask me where _____ happening!

   9. Put the food back in _____ container.

   10. The jack-in-the-box popped out of _____ box.

Write the correct homonym (*its, it's*) on the line.

   Nancy unpacked the radio from _____ box. She carefully removed
   11

_____ packaging and put the radio on _____ new stand. The
12 13

new stand was beautiful! _____ dark wood gleamed brightly. The radio looked
14

great on the top of _____ new home. "_____ awesome," she said.
15 16

Write On!

On a separate sheet of paper, write about a favorite radio, CD player, or something else that plays music. How does it work? Where do you keep it? Underline the homonyms (*its, it's*) used in the paragraph. Double-check to make sure you used the correct homonym in each sentence.

DAILY
Warm-Up 76

Root Words and Suffixes (-s, -ed, -ing)

The **root word** is the base word.

Examples: *cup, dress, lift*

A **suffix** is added to the end of the root word. A suffix changes the meaning or the tense of the word.

Example: root word + *s* (or *es*) = plural form of the word

cup + s = cups, dress + es = dresses

Example: root word + *ed* = past tense (happened already)

fill + ed = filled, lift + ed = lifted

Example: root word + *ing* = present participle verb (happening now)

dress + ing = dressing, lift + ing = lifting

PRACTICE

Write the correct form of the verb on the line.

Example: (speak) Who is <u>speaking</u> at the conference?

1. (*believe*) He _____ the story you told yesterday.

2. (*brush*) Jason is _____ his teeth.

3. (*stay*) Who is _____ to clean up?

4. (*dance*) Omar _____ at last month's recital.

5. (*work*) Liz _____ hard on her science board.

6. (*change*) Mom _____ the oil in the car.

7. (*fill*) The waiter is _____ the glasses with water.

8. (*paint*) Who _____ this gorgeous picture?

Read the paragraph. Underline the verb. Change the verbs so that they are in the same tense—past or present (happening now).

Mom and Dad planned our family vacation. They thought about going to a ghost town. We would rather go to a dude ranch. Mom and Dad were sure that we will like the ghost town. Mom is calling and is making the reservations.

WRITE ON!

On a separate sheet of paper, write a paragraph about your favorite school lunch. Check to make sure that all of the verbs are in the same tense—past or present (happening now).

Name _____ Date _____

Root Words and Suffixes (-s, -ed, -ing)

The **root word** is the base word.

 Examples: *cup, dress, lift*

A suffix is added to the end of the root word. A suffix changes the meaning or the tense of the word.

 Example: root word + *s* (or *es*) = plural form of the word

  cup + s = cups, dress + es = dresses

 Example: root word + *ed* = past tense (happened already)

  fill + ed = filled, lift + ed = lifted

 Example: root word + *ing* = present participle verb (happening now)

  dress + ing = dressing, lift + ing = lifting

Read the paragraph. Draw a line through any incorrect verb tenses. Write the correct form of the verb above the line.

 Marvin hosting his own talk show on the public access channel. During each broadcast,

Marvin interviews local dignitaries, shows film clips, and chats with kids from the local

schools. Marvin uses to have a segment where kids showing the latest skateboard moves.

It wasn't a good idea because the skateboarders had a hard time controlled the skateboards.

Many pieces of camera equipment and stage items were broken. Marvin is now thinked

of haved a segment called "Things to Cook While Playing Soccer." What do you think of

this idea?

Circle three words in the paragraph that are unfamiliar to you. Write the meaning for each of the words. If needed, use a dictionary.

 1. _____

 2. _____

 3. _____

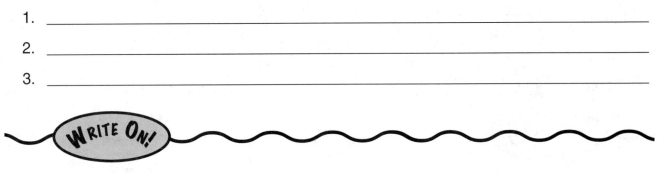

If you had your own talk show, what kinds of things would you do? What would you talk about? Whom would you interview? On a separate sheet of paper, write about your talk show.

Name _____   Date _____

Root Words and Suffixes (-s, -es)

The **root word** is the base word.

   Examples: *cup, dress, lift*

A **suffix** is added to the end of the root word. A suffix changes the meaning (or the tense) of the word.

   Example: Root word + *s* (or *es*) = plural form of the word or the third person singular
   verb tense

                    (walk) He walk<u>s</u> to school each day.

                    (run) She run<u>s</u> in marathons.

Subject-verb agreement is when both the subject and verb agree in number.

Singular (one person or item)	**Plural** (more than one person or item)
I sing.	We sing.
You sing.	They sing.
He sings.	They sing.
She sings.	They sing.
It sings.	They sing.

PRACTICE

Write the correct form of the verb on the line.

   1. (*practice*) He _____ karate every day.

   2. (*wax*) She _____ the car on weekends.

   3. (*prepare*) Dad _____ dinner on Wednesday.

   4. (*talk*) We _____ by phone every day.

   5. (*turn*) Mrs. Rice _____ on the lights at night.

   6. (*frost*) They _____ the cupcakes.

   7. (*speak*) He _____ Spanish.

   8. (*look*) Nyah and I _____ at the scoreboard.

   9. (*surf*) I _____ at the nearby beach.

   10. (*knit*) Grandma _____ for fun and relaxation.

WRITE ON!

If you were president of the United States what would you do? On a separate sheet of paper, write a paragraph answering this question. Double-check the forms of the verbs.

Vocabulary

Name _____ Date _____

Root Words and Suffixes (-s, -es)

The **root word** is the base word.

Examples: *cup, dress, lift*

A **suffix** is added to the end of the root word. A suffix changes the meaning (or the tense) of the word.

Example: Root word + *s* (or *es*) = plural form of the word or the third person singular verb tense

(walk) He walk<u>s</u> to school each day.

(run) She run<u>s</u> in marathons.

Subject-verb agreement is when both the subject and verb agree in number.

Singular (one person or item)	Plural (more than one person or item)
I sing.	We sing.
You sing.	They sing.
He sings.	They sing.
She sings.	They sing.
It sings.	They sing.

Read the paragraph checking for subject-verb agreement. Underline any sentence that does not have subject-verb agreement. On a separate piece of paper, rewrite each sentence correctly.

Jeff and Donna has an early morning paper route. Each morning, Jeff meets Donna at the local newspaper office. Together, they folds the papers and put them into their delivery bags. Then they put the delivery bags on their bikes' handlebars and are on their way. Jeff deliver the newspapers to the homes on the left side of the street. Donna delivers the newspapers to the homes on the right side of the street. They two kids is done with their route in no time!

What part of the newspaper do you enjoy reading? Why? Write a paragraph about it. On a separate sheet of paper, rewrite the paragraph changing the verb so that it is not in agreement with the subject. Exchange papers with a classmate. Underline the sentences that do not have subject-verb agreement.

Name _____   Date _____

Root Words and Suffixes (-s, -es, -ed)

The **root word** is the base word.

Examples: *cup, dress, lift*

A **suffix** is added to the end of the root word. A suffix changes the meaning (or the tense) of the word.

Example: Root word + *s* (or *es*) = present tense (happening at this time)

He fill<u>s</u> the trash can.

She listen<u>s</u> to the bird's song.

Mom fix<u>es</u> things.

Example: Root word + *ed* = past tense (happened already)

He fill<u>ed</u> the trash can.

She listen<u>ed</u> to the bird's song.

Mom fix<u>ed</u> things.

PRACTICE

Read each sentence and underline the verb. Write *present* or *past* on the line.

Example: He <u>dressed</u> carefully for the job interview.   __past__

1. She jumps over the wire. _____

2. The donkey kicked the farmer. _____

3. Baby Barney eats sloppily. _____

4. Cyrus climbs rocks for fun. _____

5. Dr. Daniels takes care of pocket pets. _____

6. Wes, Jake, and Chris liked the ice cream. _____

7. The mother catches butterflies in the net. _____

8. The truck stopped at the red light. _____

9. The dog chased the mail carrier. _____

10. Andrew helps his sister Gloria. _____

WRITE ON!

What would be the perfect job? Why? What would make it so perfect? On a separate sheet of paper, write about the job using verbs in either the present tense or the past tense. Underline the verbs used in the paragraph.

Vocabulary

Name _____ Date _____

Root Words and Suffixes (-s, -es, -ed)

The **root word** is the base word.

    Examples: *cup, dress, lift*

A **suffix** is added to the end of the root word. A suffix changes the meaning (or the tense) of the word.

    Example: Root word + *s* (or *es*) = present tense (happening at this time)

        He fill<u>s</u> the trash can.

        She listen<u>s</u> to the bird's song.

        Mom fix<u>es</u> things.

    Example: Root word + *ed* = past tense (happened already)

        He fill<u>ed</u> the trash can.

        She listen<u>ed</u> to the bird's song.

        Mom fix<u>ed</u> things.

Read each paragraph. Underline the verb in each sentence.

> Katy climbs mountains on the weekend. On Friday night, Katy checks her climbing equipment to make sure that she has everything she needs: helmet, shoes, ropes, backpack, water, snacks, first-aid kit, and a change of clothes. In the morning, Katy rides her bike to the nearby mountain and begins climbing. One day, she hopes to scale the tallest mountains in the world.
>
> What tense are all of the verbs? _____

> Katy climbed mountains on the weekend. On Friday night, Katy checked her climbing equipment to make sure that she had everything she needed: helmet, shoes, ropes, backpack, water, snacks, first-aid kit, and a change of clothes. In the morning, Katy rode her bike to the nearby mountain and began climbing. One day, she hoped to scale the tallest mountains in the world.
>
> What tense are all of the verbs? _____

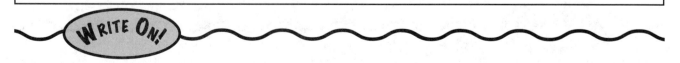

WRITE ON!

Would you like to go mountain climbing? Why or why not? On a separate sheet of paper, write about this topic and underline the verbs used in the paragraph. Are they all in the same tense? If not, change the necessary verbs so that all of the tenses match.

Name _____   Date _____

Syllables (Prefix re-, Suffix -ful)

Every word has at least one **syllable**. Each syllable must have a vowel sound. The vowel can be by itself or combined with one or more consonants.

Word	Syllables	Vowel Sounds	Number of Syllable
a	a	one vowel sound	one syllable
apple	ap/ple	two vowel sounds	two syllables
idea	i/de/a	three vowel sounds	three syllables

Before dividing a word into syllables, check the word for prefixes or suffixes. Underline the base word. Divide the word between the prefix or suffix and the base word.

Example: rewash   re/<u>wash</u>   The prefix is *re–*, and the base word is *wash*.

PRACTICE

Underline the base word. Divide the word between the base word and its prefix or suffix. Write the number of syllables and the meaning of the word. Remember that the prefix *re–* means again and the suffix *–ful* means full of.

Word	Syllables	Number of Syllables	Meaning of the Word
Example: rewash	re/<u>wash</u>	2	to wash again

1. redo _____ _____ _____

2. reread _____ _____ _____

3. refill _____ _____ _____

4. remade _____ _____ _____

5. replay _____ _____ _____

6. playful _____ _____ _____

7. cheerful _____ _____ _____

8. eyeful _____ _____ _____

9. tasteful _____ _____ _____

10. frightful _____ _____ _____

WRITE ON!

On a separate sheet of paper, write several sentences using words with prefixes or suffixes. Exchange papers with a classmate. Underline the prefixes and suffixes used in the paragraph. At the bottom of the page, write the meaning of the underlined words.

Vocabulary

Name _____ Date _____

Syllables (Prefixes un-, pre- and Suffixes -less, -er)

Every word has at least one **syllable**. Each syllable must have a vowel sound. The vowel can be by itself or combined with one or more consonants.

Word	Syllables	Vowel Sounds	Number of Syllable
a	a	one vowel sound	one syllable
apple	ap/ple	two vowel sounds	two syllables
idea	i/de/a	three vowel sounds	three syllables

Before dividing a word into syllables, check the word for prefixes or suffixes. Underline the base word. Divide the word between the prefix or suffix and the base word.

Example: unwash   un/<u>wash</u>   The prefix is *un*, and the base word is *wash*.

PRACTICE

Underline the base word. Divide the word between the base word and its prefix or suffix. Write the number of syllables and the meaning of the word.

	Prefixes	Suffixes	
	un = not	*less* = without	
	pre = before	*er* = person who does this	

Word	Syllables	Number of Syllables	Meaning of the Word
Example: un<u>wash</u>	un/wash	2	Not washed
1. unhappy _____	_____	_____
2. pretest _____	_____	_____
3. preview _____	_____	_____
4. meatless _____	_____	_____
5. ageless _____	_____	_____
6. player _____	_____	_____
7. driver _____	_____	_____
8. weightless _____	_____	_____

WRITE ON!

Have you ever not studied for a test? What happened? What did you learn from that experience? On a separate sheet of paper, write a paragraph about this and underline the words that have a prefix or a suffix.

Vocabulary

Name _____ Date _____

Syllables (Compound Words)

Every word has at least one **syllable**. Each syllable must have a vowel sound. The vowel can be by itself or combined with one or more consonants.

Word	Syllables	Vowel Sounds	Number of Syllable
a	a	one vowel sound	one syllable
apple	ap/ple	two vowel sounds	two syllables
idea	i/de/a	three vowel sounds	three syllables

Before dividing a word into syllables, check the word for prefixes or suffixes. For example, in the word *overcook*, the prefix is *over* and the base word is *cook*.

Underline the base word. Divide the word between the base word and its prefix or suffix. Write the number of syllables and the meaning of the word.

Prefixes	Suffixes
over = done, to exceed	*ness* = state of being
mid = middle	*ish* = like

Word	Syllables	Number of Syllables	Meaning of the Word
Example: over<u>cook</u>	o/ver/cook	3	cooked too much

1. overbid _____ _____ _____

2. loneliness _____ _____ _____

3. midcourse _____ _____ _____

4. impish _____ _____ _____

5. replay _____ _____ _____

6. childish _____ _____ _____

7. midday _____ _____ _____

8. sadness _____ _____ _____

9. midlife _____ _____ _____

WRITE ON!

On a separate sheet of paper, write about a cooking disaster you have had. What were you making? What went wrong? Did you ever try making it again? Underline any words that have a prefix or suffix. Then divide the underlined words into syllables.

Name _____   Date _____

DAILY
Warm-Up 85

Syllables (Prefixes and Suffixes)

Every word has at least one **syllable**. Each syllable must have a vowel sound. The vowel can be by itself or combined with one or more consonants.

Word	Syllables	Vowel Sounds	Number of Syllable
a	a	one vowel sound	one syllable
apple	ap/ple	two vowel sounds	two syllables
idea	i/de/a	three vowel sounds	three syllables

Before dividing a word into syllables, check the word for prefixes or suffixes. Underline the base word. Divide the word between the prefix or suffix and the base word.

Example: unneeded   un/<u>need</u>/ed

This word has both a prefix and a suffix.

PRACTICE

Underline the base word and divide the word into syllables.

1. unknowing _____

2. distasteful _____

3. unlikely _____

4. hopefully _____

5. unfriendly _____

6. unending _____

7. cheerfully _____

8. rechecking _____

Read the paragraph. Underline the words that have three syllables.

   Ernie runs the corner grocery store. He sells many things at the store. Besides candy,

slush drinks, and sugar sticks, Ernie also sells food items, cleaning supplies, and magazines.

Ernie keeps his store spotless and always greets the customers with a smile.

WRITE ON!

What kinds of things do you like to do with your friends? On a separate sheet of paper, write about this topic. Use at least two prefixes and two suffixes in your paragraph. Trade papers with a classmate. Underline the prefixes and suffixes used.

Name _____   Date _____

Syllables (Prefixes and Suffixes)

Every word has at least one **syllable**. Each syllable must have a vowel sound. The vowel can be by itself or combined with one or more consonants.

Word	Syllables	Vowel Sounds	Number of Syllable
a	a	one vowel sound	one syllable
apple	ap/ple	two vowel sounds	two syllables
idea	i/de/a	three vowel sounds	three syllables

Before dividing a word into syllables, check the word for prefixes or suffixes. Underline the base word. Divide the word between the prefix or suffix and the base word.

   Example: unneeded   un/<u>need</u>/ed

This word has both a prefix and a suffix.

Check to see if each word is correctly divided into syllables. If not, correctly divide the word into its syllables.

1. happiness   hap/pi/ness _____

2. repayment   repay/ment_____

3. unforgettable   unfor/get/ta/ble_____

4. relapse   re/lapse _____

5. messiness   mes/si/ness _____

6. sadness   sadn/ess _____

7. refinishing   re/finish/ing _____

8. unbelievable   un/be/lie/va/ble_____

9. unable   un/able_____

10. rewrite   re/write_____

11. remaking   re/mak/ing _____

12. regrouping   re/grou/ping _____

On a separate sheet of paper, write about a time when you were unhappy. What happened to make you feel that way? Underline the words that use a prefix or a suffix in the paragraph.

Name _____ Date _____

Syllables (VC/CV)

Every word has at least one **syllable**. Each syllable must have a vowel sound. The vowel can be by itself or combined with one or more consonants.

Word	Syllables	Vowel Sounds	Number of Syllable
a	a	one vowel sound	one syllable
apple	ap/ple	two vowel sounds	two syllables
idea	i/de/a	three vowel sounds	three syllables

Before dividing a word into syllables, check for multiple consonants between vowels. Divide the word between the consonants.

VC/CV (Vowel-Consonant-Consonant-Vowel)

Examples: b<u>att</u>er = bat/ter   b<u>utt</u>er = but/ter

PRACTICE

Underline the VCCV pattern in each word. Divide the word into syllables.

Example: b<u>ett</u>er   bet/ter

1. stapler _____
2. blanket _____
3. pillow _____
4. window _____
5. curtain _____
6. hollow _____
7. candy _____
8. pencil _____
9. marker _____
10. slipper _____

11. mirror _____
12. puppy _____
13. kitten _____
14. pasture _____
15. carpet _____
16. monkey _____
17. rabbit _____
18. button _____
19. torso _____
20. mitten _____

Write three more words that fit the VCCV pattern.

_____ , _____ , _____

WRITE ON!

On a separate sheet of paper, write about your favorite restaurant. What is it that you like about the food? Underline the words that fit the VCCV pattern.

Syllables (VC/CV)

Every word has at least one **syllable**. Each syllable must have a vowel sound. The vowel can be by itself or combined with one or more consonants.

Word	Syllables	Vowel Sounds	Number of Syllable
a	a	one vowel sound	one syllable
apple	ap/ple	two vowel sounds	two syllables
idea	i/de/a	three vowel sounds	three syllables

Before dividing a word into syllables, check for multiple consonants between vowels. Divide the word between the consonants.

VC/CV (Vowel-Consonant-Consonant-Vowel)

Examples: b<u>atte</u>r = bat/ter   b<u>utte</u>r = but/ter

Read the paragraph. Underline the words that fit the VCCV pattern.

   Margene is taking an auto repair class. She studies all kinds of things about cars. In the first class, the students learned the names for the different parts outside of the car: tires, hubcaps, trunk, hood, roof, door, window, and gas cap. This week, the students will study about what is under the hood. Margene was amazed at all of the parts that are needed to make a car actually drive.

Write the VCCV words on the line. Divide each word into its syllables.

1. _____   5. _____

2. _____   6. _____

3. _____   7. _____

4. _____

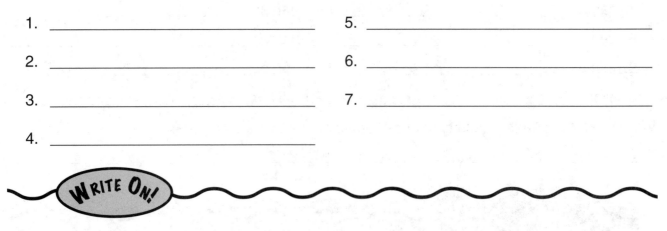

Have you ever tried something new? On a separate sheet of paper, write a paragraph about the experience. Exchange papers with a classmate. Underline the VCCV words used in the story.

Name _____ Date _____

Syllables (V/CV)

Every word has at least one **syllable**. Each syllable must have a vowel sound. The vowel can be by itself or combined with one or more consonants.

Word	Syllables	Vowel Sounds	Number of Syllable
a	a	one vowel sound	one syllable
apple	ap/ple	two vowel sounds	two syllables
idea	i/de/a	three vowel sounds	three syllables

Before dividing a word into syllables, look at the vowel. If the vowel is long (it says its name), divide the word after the vowel. These are also known as *open syllables*. An open syllable is when the last element in the syllable is a vowel sound.

V/CV (Vowel-Consonant-Vowel)

Example: <u>la</u>ter   la/ter

PRACTICE

Look at each word. Underline the VCV pattern. If the vowel is long, divide the word after the vowel.

Example: <u>ba</u>ker   ba/ker

1. tuna _____
2. motel _____
3. remote _____
4. paper _____
5. color _____
6. solid _____
7. erase _____
8. iris _____

9. lily _____
10. satin _____
11. lilac _____
12. medic _____
13. pirate _____
14. unique _____
15. shady _____
16. pony _____

Read the paragraph. Underline the words that fit the VCV pattern and have a long vowel.

Michael loves to work on vintage cars. His favorite car is an old green one that his

grandpa used to drive. Michael has overhauled the engine, painted the outside of the car,

and put in a brand-new leather interior. It's a beautiful car!

WRITE ON!

Have you ever made something look brand-new? On a separate sheet of paper, write about the experience. Exchange papers with a classmate. Underline the words that fit the VCV pattern and have a long vowel.

Name _____   Date _____

Syllables (V/CV)

Every word has at least one **syllable**. Each syllable must have a vowel sound. The vowel can be by itself or combined with one or more consonants.

Word	Syllables	Vowel Sounds	Number of Syllable
a	a	one vowel sound	one syllable
apple	ap/ple	two vowel sounds	two syllables
idea	i/de/a	three vowel sounds	three syllables

Before dividing a word into syllables, look at the vowel. If the vowel is long (it says its name), divide the word after the vowel. These are also known as *open syllables*. An open syllable is when the last element in the syllable is a vowel sound.

V/CV (Vowel-Consonant-Vowel)

Example: <u>la</u>ter   la/ter

PRACTICE

Read the paragraph and underline the words that fit the V/CV pattern (have an open vowel sound).

    Our family has a dog named Rufus. Rufus is a pedigree. Over the weekend, Rufus entered a national dog show. He was so excited to be in the center ring and have everyone's eyes on him. Rufus showed his stuff. He strutted around the ring, struck his poses, and followed all of his commands. Rufus didn't win first place, but he did win the runner-up position.

Write the words that fit the V/CV pattern (and have an open vowel sound) on the lines. Divide each word into its syllables.

1. _____   3. _____

2. _____   4. _____

WRITE ON!

Have you ever been to a show or a competition? What kinds of things were being shown? How was the winner picked? Which one did you think was best? On a separate sheet of paper, write all about the show or competition. Exchange papers with a classmate. Underline the words that fit the VCV pattern and have a long vowel.

Name _____ Date _____

Syllables (VC/V)

Every word has at least one **syllable**. Each syllable must have a vowel sound. The vowel can be by itself or combined with one or more consonants.

Word	Syllables	Vowel Sounds	Number of Syllable
a	a	one vowel sound	one syllable
apple	ap/ple	two vowel sounds	two syllables
idea	i/de/a	three vowel sounds	three syllables

Before dividing a word into syllables, look at the vowel. If the vowel is short, divide the word after the consonant. These are also known as *closed syllables*. A closed syllable is when the last element in the syllable is a consonant sound.

VC/V (Vowel-Consonant-Vowel)

Example: <u>tal</u>ent   tal/ent

PRACTICE

Look at each word. Underline the VCV pattern. If the vowel is short, divide the word after the consonant.

Example: <u>sol</u>id   sol/id

1. color _____
2. gravel _____
3. lily _____
4. shady _____
5. pony _____
6. garish _____
7. shovel _____
8. limit _____

9. image _____
10. cavern _____
11. closet _____
12. frolic _____
13. olive _____
14. vacant _____
15. famish _____
16. hotel _____

Read the paragraph. Underline the words that fit the VCV pattern and have a short vowel.

Heidi has a new dog. The dog's name was Lovie, but Heidi changed it to Lily. She thought

Lily was a better fit. Lily is a white color. She loves to have her soft fur brushed and her ears

cleaned. Her chew toy is made of linen. She hides it in the closet. Lily is the best dog!

WRITE ON!

In your opinion what makes a great dog? On a separate sheet of paper, write about this topic. Exchange papers with a classmate. Underline the words that fit the VCV pattern and have a short vowel.

Name _____ Date _____

Syllables (VC/V)

Every word has at least one **syllable**. Each syllable must have a vowel sound. The vowel can be by itself or combined with one or more consonants.

Word	Syllables	Vowel Sounds	Number of Syllable
a	a	one vowel sound	one syllable
apple	ap/ple	two vowel sounds	two syllables
idea	i/de/a	three vowel sounds	three syllables

Before dividing a word into syllables, look at the vowel. If the vowel is short, divide the word after the consonant. These are also known as *closed syllables*. A closed syllable is when the last element in the syllable is a consonant sound.

VC/V (Vowel-Consonant-Vowel)

Example: ta<u>le</u>nt   tal/ent

PRACTICE

Underline the words that fit the VC/V pattern.

   Billy was so excited. Today was his seventh birthday. For breakfast, his mom made pancakes with syrup. Billy's pancakes spelled out his name. For lunch, his dad took him to the local pizza place. Billy ordered pepperoni pizza with chili peppers. For dinner, his grandparents came over. Grandpa barbecued hot dogs. After dinner, Billy got to blow out the candles on his birthday cake. It was devil's food cake with lemon frosting. It was a great day!

On the lines, write the VCV words. Then divide each word into its syllables.

1. _____   4. _____

2. _____   5. _____

3. _____

WRITE ON!

On a separate sheet of paper, write a paragraph describing the best birthday dessert. Exchange papers with a classmate. Underline the words that fit the VC/V pattern.

Syllables (Consonant + le)

Every word has at least one **syllable**. Each syllable must have a vowel sound. The vowel can be by itself or combined with one or more consonants.

Word	Syllables	Vowel Sounds	Number of Syllable
a	a	one vowel sound	one syllable
apple	ap/ple	two vowel sounds	two syllables
idea	i/de/a	three vowel sounds	three syllables

Before dividing a word into syllables, look to see if the word ends in a **consonant + le**. The consonant + *le* forms the final syllable in the word.

   Example: bicy<u>cle</u>   bi/cy/cle

The exception to this rule is if the word has a *ck* before the *le*. Divide the word between the *ck* and the *le*.

   Example: ti<u>ckle</u>   tick/le

PRACTICE

Look at each word. Find the consonant + *le* pattern. Divide the word <u>before</u> the consonant + *le*.

   Example: able   a/ble

1. icicle _____
2. fumble _____
3. rubble _____
4. mumble _____
5. stumble _____
6. recycle _____
7. cycle _____
8. bumble _____
9. rumble _____
10. tumble _____

11. pickle _____
12. trickle _____
13. purple _____
14. little _____
15. uncle _____
16. idle _____
17. apple _____
18. turtle _____
19. bubble _____
20. eagle _____

WRITE ON!

On a separate sheet of paper, write all the facts you know about an octopus. Underline the words that fit the consonant + *le* pattern.

Name _____   Date _____

Syllables (Consonant + le)

Every word has at least one **syllable**. Each syllable must have a vowel sound. The vowel can be by itself or combined with one or more consonants.

Word	Syllables	Vowel Sounds	Number of Syllable
a	a	one vowel sound	one syllable
apple	ap/ple	two vowel sounds	two syllables
idea	i/de/a	three vowel sounds	three syllables

Before dividing a word into syllables, look to see if the word ends in a **consonant + le**. The consonant + le forms the final syllable in the word.

   Example: bicycle   bi/cy/cle

The exception to this rule is if the word has a *ck* before the *le*. Divide the word between the *ck* and the *le*.

   Example: tickle   tick/le

PRACTICE

Read the paragraph. Underline the words that fit the rule.

   My favorite hobby is metal detecting. I like to go metal detecting at my favorite place. It's near the castle. It's not really a castle anymore. It's just a bunch of rubble. But it looks like it might have been a castle at one time. Last time I went metal detecting, I found a nickel, a purple turtle made from metal, and a horn from a tricycle. While I haven't found anything worth a lot yet, I still like the thrill of the hunt.

Write the words on the lines. Use each word only once. Then divide each word into its syllables.

1. _____   4. _____

2. _____   5. _____

3. _____

WRITE ON!

On a separate sheet of paper, write a paragraph telling what you would do if you found a valuable item. Underline the words that fit the rule. At the bottom of the page, divide each word into its syllables.

Name _____ Date _____

Syllables (Compound Words)

Every word has at least one **syllable**. Each syllable must have a vowel sound. The vowel can be by itself or combined with one or more consonants.

Word	Syllables	Vowel Sounds	Number of Syllable
a	a	one vowel sound	one syllable
apple	ap/ple	two vowel sounds	two syllables
idea	i/de/a	three vowel sounds	three syllables

Before dividing a word into its syllables, check to see if it is a **compound word**. If it is, divide the compound word between its two parts.

   Example: cornbread   corn/bread

Read each sentence and underline the compound word. Divide the compound word into its syllables.

   Example: I can't find the <u>baseball</u>.   _base/ball_

1. When I grow up I want to be a firefighter. _____
2. Do you want to make a snowman? _____
3. To keep my neck warm, I wear turtlenecks. _____
4. Tina ate two pieces of watermelon at the park. _____
5. Where is Grandma? _____
6. Do you know how to use a keyboard? _____
7. We went downstairs to the basement. _____
8. A spider has eight eyeballs. _____

Read the paragraph. Underline the compound words.

   When I grow up I want to be a secret agent. I am really good at wearing disguises and going undercover. I always wear an overcoat with many pockets. In the pockets, I keep the many tools I need in order to do my job well. I carry a spyglass, funny eyeglasses, a pair of overalls, and some socks. When spying on somebody, I never ring the doorbell. Instead, I peek into windows or follow them on my motorcycle. I will be a fantastic secret agent!

Think of a secret agent you might have read about or seen on a TV show or movie. On a separate sheet of paper, write everything you know about the secret agent. Exchange papers with a classmate. Underline the compound words used in the paragraph.

Name _____   Date _____

Syllables (Compound Words)

Every word has at least one **syllable**. Each syllable must have a vowel sound. The vowel can be by itself or combined with one or more consonants.

Word	Syllables	Vowel Sounds	Number of Syllable
a	a	one vowel sound	one syllable
apple	ap/ple	two vowel sounds	two syllables
idea	i/de/a	three vowel sounds	three syllables

Before dividing a word into its syllables, check to see if it is a **compound word**. If it is, divide the compound word between its two parts.

Example: cornbread   corn/bread

Read the paragraph. Underline the compound words.

    Our troop took a boat out onto the ocean. The boat was unique, because it had a glass bottom. Through the glass bottom, our troop could see all of the amazing sea creatures. Gary saw a seahorse. It was very unusual looking. The twins said that they saw a hammerhead shark, but the troop leader said that it was a jellyfish. The twins said that they were confused, because they weren't wearing their eyeglasses. Steve saw an octopus with its eggs. The eggs looked like little rainbows. We had a great time at the seaside.

Write the compound words on the line. Divide each word into its syllables.

1. _____   4. _____

2. _____   5. _____

3. _____   6. _____

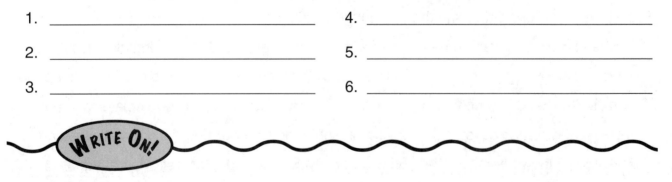

On a separate sheet of paper, write a paragraph about animals that live in the sea. Exchange papers with a classmate. Have the classmate underline the compound words used in the paragraph.

Name _____ Date _____

Syllables (ck, x)

Every word has at least one **syllable**. Each syllable must have a vowel sound. The vowel can be by itself or combined with one or more consonants.

Word	Syllables	Vowel Sounds	Number of Syllable
a	a	one vowel sound	one syllable
apple	ap/ple	two vowel sounds	two syllables
idea	i/de/a	three vowel sounds	three syllables

If a word has a *ck* or an *x*, divide the word after the *ck* or the *x*.

Examples: chi<u>ck</u>en   chick/en   ta<u>x</u>i   tax/i

PRACTICE

Read each sentence and underline the word that fits the pattern. Divide the word into its syllables.

Example: The mail carrier delivered the <u>package</u>.   <u>pack/age</u>

1. The fans were told not to heckle the players. _____

2. Grandma always wears the locket Grandpa gave her. _____

3. Do you have the tackle box? _____

4. I'll give you a nickel for every correct answer. _____

5. Stop tickling the baby! _____

6. Let's play checkers. _____

7. I am mixing the cookie dough. _____

8. Do you know how to play sixes and sevens? _____

9. The secretary is faxing over the paperwork. _____

10. What is the maximum weight the truck can carry? _____

11. Did you get the tickets? _____

12. I was lost in the thicket. _____

13. The oxen are in the pasture. _____

14. The lumberjack sharpened the axes. _____

15. To thicken the soup, add more flour to the pot. _____

WRITE ON!

On a separate sheet of paper, write the rules for checkers or describe the game itself. Underline the words that fit the "rule" above. Write the words at the bottom of the page and divide each word into its syllables.

Name _____ Date _____

Syllables (ck, x)

Every word has at least one **syllable**. Each syllable must have a vowel sound. The vowel can be by itself or combined with one or more consonants.

Word	Syllables	Vowel Sounds	Number of Syllable
a	a	one vowel sound	one syllable
apple	ap/ple	two vowel sounds	two syllables
idea	i/de/a	three vowel sounds	three syllables

If a word has a *ck* or an *x*, divide the word after the *ck* or the *x*.

Examples: chicken   chick/en   taxi   tax/i

PRACTICE

Read the paragraph. Underline the words that fit the rule.

   When my dad was in college, he drove a taxi to pay the bills. His taxi took people from all over the world. He drove them to both new and old parts of the city. My dad was tickled to learn how to greet people in over thirty different languages. One fare even gave him a nickel for every greeting that my dad said. My dad was lucky. He never once had an accident or was given a ticket while driving the taxi.

Write the words that fit the rule. Use each word only once. Divide each word into its syllables.

1. _____

2. _____

3. _____

4. _____

5. _____

WRITE ON!

On a separate sheet of paper, write a paragraph about being a taxi driver. When could the job be dangerous? What would make the job fun and exciting? Underline the words that fit the rule.

Name _____ Date _____

Syllables (Two Vowels Together)

Every word has at least one **syllable**. Each syllable must have a vowel sound. The vowel can be by itself or combined with one or more consonants.

Word	Syllables	Vowel Sounds	Number of Syllable
a	a	one vowel sound	one syllable
apple	ap/ple	two vowel sounds	two syllables
idea	i/de/a	three vowel sounds	three syllables

When two vowels are together in a word <u>and each one makes its own sound</u>, divide the word between the two vowels.

Example: rad<u>io</u>   ra/di/o

PRACTICE

Underline the two vowels in the word. If each vowel makes its own sound, divide the word between the two vowels. Show all the syllables in the words below.

Example: br<u>ui</u>n   bru/in

1. sleeve _____
2. lotion _____
3. head _____
4. being _____
5. void _____
6. coin _____
7. violent _____
8. lion _____

9. green _____
10. guitar _____
11. floor _____
12. leather _____
13. diet _____
14. factual _____
15. video _____
16. iota _____

Read the paragraph. Underline any misspelled words. Write the correct spelling of the word above it.

Brian just started taking gutar lessons from his friend Larry. At the beginning of each lesson, Brian watches a vidyo that shows the correct finger positions. Brian picks up his guitar and puts the leather strap around his neck. Then Brian strums the strings and makes a lot of noyse. After he is done beeing a rock star, the actuel lesson begins.

WRITE ON!

Have you ever taken lessons to learn how to play an instrument? On a separate sheet of paper, write a paragraph telling about the lessons.

Name _____   Date _____

Syllables (Two Vowels Together)

Every word has at least one **syllable**. Each syllable must have a vowel sound. The vowel can be by itself or combined with one or more consonants.

Word	Syllables	Vowel Sounds	Number of Syllable
a	a	one vowel sound	one syllable
apple	ap/ple	two vowel sounds	two syllables
idea	i/de/a	three vowel sounds	three syllables

When two vowels are together in a word <u>and each one makes its own sound</u>, divide the word between the two vowels.

Example: rad<u>io</u>   ra/di/o

Read the paragraph. Underline the words that fit the rule.

　　Our school is participating in the fitness challenge. We met at the stadium to get weighed in before the competition began. As part of the competition, we will watch our diet. Most of us will start eating cereal for breakfast. Our parents are actually surprised that we are willing to give up junk food.

Divide each word into its syllables.

1. _____   3. _____

2. _____   4. _____

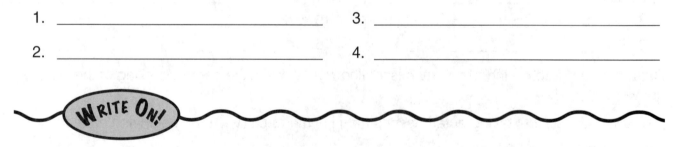

There has been a lot of news about how out of shape people are, especially kids. What do you do to stay in shape? On a separate sheet of paper, write about this issue. Underline any words that have two vowels together in a word and each vowel makes its own sound.

Name _____ Date _____

Syllables (Vowel Forms Its Own Syllable)

Every word has at least one **syllable**. Each syllable must have a vowel sound. The vowel can be by itself or combined with one or more consonants.

Word	Syllables	Vowel Sounds	Number of Syllable
a	a	one vowel sound	one syllable
apple	ap/ple	two vowel sounds	two syllables
idea	i/de/a	three vowel sounds	three syllables

When a vowel is sounded alone in a word, it forms its own syllable.

Example: grad<u>u</u>ate   grad/u/ate

Underline the word in each sentence that fits the rule. Divide the word into its syllables.

1. Do you know the names of all of the elements?   _____

2. I have a new digital clock.   _____

3. The elephant is a very large land mammal.   _____

4. You are a mathematical genius!   _____

5. Have you ever tried caviar?   _____

6. The hyena is a very strange creature.   _____

7. Emily's favorite animal is the pig.   _____

8. Christina has the privilege of driving the car.   _____

9. Grandma finished her manuscript.   _____

10. Manny is very flexible for a swimmer.   _____

Write three other words that fit this rule.

_____ , _____ , _____

Have you ever been lost? On a separate sheet of paper, write about the experience. Exchange papers with a classmate. Underline the words that fit the rule.

Name _____ Date _____

Syllables (Vowel Forms Its Own Syllable)

Every word has at least one **syllable**. Each syllable must have a vowel sound. The vowel can be by itself or combined with one or more consonants.

Word	Syllables	Vowel Sounds	Number of Syllable
a	a	one vowel sound	one syllable
apple	ap/ple	two vowel sounds	two syllables
idea	i/de/a	three vowel sounds	three syllables

When a vowel is sounded alone in a word, it forms its own syllable.

   Example: grad<u>u</u>ate   grad/u/ate

PRACTICE

Read the paragraph. Underline the words that fit the rule.

   Olivia is a creative person. She once made a chrysalis out of flexible wire and tissue

paper. She then made the animal it would become, a butterfly, using similar materials. Olivia

then made their habitat including all of the important elements: plants, nectar, grass, sun,

and water. It was a beautiful exhibit.

Divide each word into its syllables. Use each word only once.

1. _____   5. _____

2. _____   6. _____

3. _____   7. _____

4. _____   8. _____

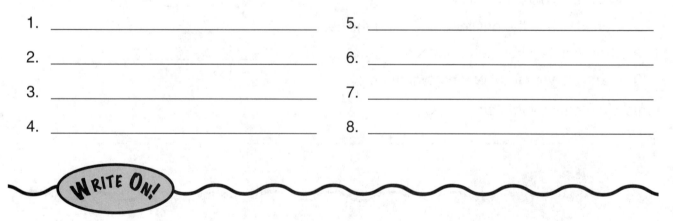

WRITE ON!

On a separate sheet of paper, describe a butterfly. What does it look like? What colors are on its wings and body? Exchange papers with a classmate. Underline the words that fit the rule.

Name _____   Date _____

Syllables (be, de, ex, re)

Every word has at least one **syllable**. Each syllable must have a vowel sound. The vowel can be by itself or combined with one or more consonants.

Word	Syllables	Vowel Sounds	Number of Syllable
a	a	one vowel sound	one syllable
apple	ap/ple	two vowel sounds	two syllables
idea	i/de/a	three vowel sounds	three syllables

When *be, de, ex,* or *re* are at the beginning of a word, they make a syllable of their own.

Example: <u>be</u>cause   be/cause

PRACTICE

Divide the word into its syllables.

Example: delay   <u>de/lay</u>

1. repeat _____

2. defend _____

3. exit _____

4. exhale _____

5. replay _____

6. recycle _____

7. explore _____

8. excuse _____

9. recall_____

10. expo _____

11. exercise _____

12. detail _____

13. remade _____

14. extinct _____

15. beneath _____

16. expand _____

17. design _____

18. befriend _____

19. rebuild _____

20. exceed _____

Write three other words that fit this rule.

_____, _____, _____

WRITE ON!

Why is it important to recycle? On a separate sheet of paper, write about this topic. Underline the words the fit the rule.

Vocabulary

Name _____   Date _____

Syllables (be, de, ex, re)

Every word has at least one **syllable**. Each syllable must have a vowel sound. The vowel can be by itself or combined with one or more consonants.

Word	Syllables	Vowel Sounds	Number of Syllable
a	a	one vowel sound	one syllable
apple	ap/ple	two vowel sounds	two syllables
idea	i/de/a	three vowel sounds	three syllables

When *be, de, ex,* or *re* are at the beginning of a word, they make a syllable of their own.

Example: <u>be</u>cause   be/cause

PRACTICE

Read the paragraph. Underline the words that fit the rule.

   Joshua likes to exercise every day. He says he does it because it feels good and helps him to relax after a hard day at school. When he begins his exercises, he warms up with a few stretches. Then he decides if he is going to go jogging, run on the treadmill, or jump on the trampoline. He stops exercising when he feels exhausted. Then he drinks plenty of water so that he doesn't become dehydrated.

Divide each word into its syllables.

1. _____   6. _____

2. _____   7. _____

3. _____   8. _____

4. _____   9. _____

5. _____   10. _____

WRITE ON!

What kind of exercising do you like to do? How does it make you feel when you are doing the exercise? On a separate sheet of paper, write about this topic. Underline the words that fit the rule.

Name _____ Date _____

Syllables (-ed)

Every word has at least one **syllable**. Each syllable must have a vowel sound. The vowel can be by itself or combined with one or more consonants.

Word	Syllables	Vowel Sounds	Number of Syllable
a	a	one vowel sound	one syllable
apple	ap/ple	two vowel sounds	two syllables
idea	i/de/a	three vowel sounds	three syllables

When –*ed* comes at the end of the word and follows a /t/ or /d/ sound, it forms its own syllable.

Example: start<u>ed</u>   start/ed

PRACTICE

If the suffix –*ed* follows a /t/ or /d/ sound, divide the word into its syllables.

1. acted _____
2. promised _____
3. captured _____
4. squinted _____
5. parted _____
6. dented _____
7. printed _____
8. looked _____
9. used _____
10. tasted _____

11. heated _____
12. footed _____
13. crowded _____
14. squirted _____
15. lighted _____
16. talked _____
17. rated _____
18. loaded _____
19. fainted _____
20. darted _____

Write three other words that fit this rule.

_____, _____, _____

WRITE ON!

Pretend you met a three-footed alien. On a separate sheet of paper, write about the experience. Underline the words that fit this rule.

Vocabulary

Name _____   Date _____

Syllables (-ed)

Every word has at least one **syllable**. Each syllable must have a vowel sound. The vowel can be by itself or combined with one or more consonants.

Word	Syllables	Vowel Sounds	Number of Syllable
a	a	one vowel sound	one syllable
apple	ap/ple	two vowel sounds	two syllables
idea	i/de/a	three vowel sounds	three syllables

When *–ed* comes at the end of the word and follows a /t/ or /d/ sound, it forms its own syllable.

   Example: start<u>ed</u>   start/ed

PRACTICE

Read the paragraph. Underline the words that fit the rule.

   During vacation, my family and I went camping. We stayed in tents and attempted to live off of the land. Each day we went out fishing. We took our boat out onto the pond and just floated on the water. Most of the time we didn't catch any fish, so Mom heated up cans of soup and made cornbread over the campfire. At night, Mom and Dad tucked us into our sleeping bags and wished us sweet dreams. But I always dreamed of bears chasing me to get to my secret stash of candy bars!

Divide each word into its syllables.

   1. _____   3. _____

   2. _____

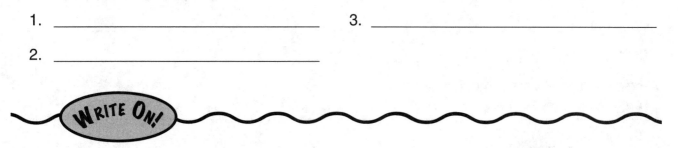

WRITE ON!

What kinds of things would you like to do if you went camping? On a separate sheet of paper, write a paragraph answering this question. Underline any words where *–ed* comes at the end of the word and follows a /t/ or /d/ sound.

Syllables (-al, -el)

Every word has at least one **syllable**. Each syllable must have a vowel sound. The vowel can be by itself or combined with one or more consonants.

Word	Syllables	Vowel Sounds	Number of Syllable
a	a	one vowel sound	one syllable
apple	ap/ple	two vowel sounds	two syllables
idea	i/de/a	three vowel sounds	three syllables

When a word ends in –al or –el, these letters usually make the final syllable in the word.

Example: usu<u>al</u>   us/u/al

PRACTICE

Divide the word into its syllable if the word ends in –al or –el. Use a dictionary if needed.

1. level _____
2. model _____
3. portal _____
4. regal _____
5. feral _____
6. cruel _____
7. herbal _____
8. laurel _____
9. mutual _____
10. pedal _____

11. mental _____
12. petal _____
13. legal _____
14. total _____
15. gruel _____
16. habitual _____
17. floral _____
18. jewel _____
19. nickel _____
20. medal _____

Write three words that rhyme with *legal*.

_____, _____, _____

What do you notice about their spellings? Do the words fit the rule?

_____

WRITE ON!

What would be the perfect dog? On a separate sheet of paper, write a paragraph answering this question. Use some of the words from above to tell about the perfect dog. Underline the words that fit the rule. Use a dictionary if needed.

Name _____ Date _____

Syllables (-al, -el)

Every word has at least one **syllable**. Each syllable must have a vowel sound. The vowel can be by itself or combined with one or more consonants.

Word	Syllables	Vowel Sounds	Number of Syllable
a	a	one vowel sound	one syllable
apple	ap/ple	two vowel sounds	two syllables
idea	i/de/a	three vowel sounds	three syllables

When a word ends in _-al_ or _-el_, these letters usually make the final syllable in the word.

Example: usu<u>al</u>   us/u/al

Read the paragraph. Underline the words that fit the rule.

    For Halloween, we dressed up in our usual costumes. My sister went as a model. My brother went as a legal wiz. I went as a daisy, complete with a million petals. Once we had our novel costumes on, our dad took us out trick-or-treating. Our first stop was Old Man Greer's house. He always gives out nickels instead of candy. He said that I should be in a floral display and that my brother should win a medal for being a lawyer. By mutual agreement, our next stop was Mrs. Jewel's house. She gives out the best treats! By the end of the evening, our bags were full of candy, and we were tired!

Divide each word into its syllables.

1. _____   6. _____

2. _____   7. _____

3. _____   8. _____

4. _____   9. _____

5. _____   10. _____

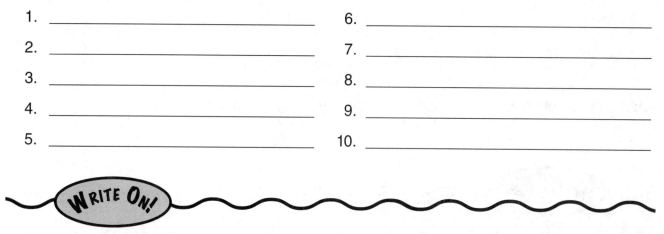

Do you go trick-or-treating? What was your favorite costume and why? On a separate sheet of paper, write a paragraph answering these questions. Underline any words that follow the rule above.

Name _____ Date _____

Syllables (-ture, -tion)

Every word has at least one **syllable**. Each syllable must have a vowel sound. The vowel can be by itself or combined with one or more consonants.

Word	Syllables	Vowel Sounds	Number of Syllable
a	a	one vowel sound	one syllable
apple	ap/ple	two vowel sounds	two syllables
idea	i/de/a	three vowel sounds	three syllables

When –ture or –tion is at the end of a word, it forms its own syllable.

    Example: na<u>tion</u>   na/tion

Divide the word into syllables.

1. station _____
2. stature _____
3. creation _____
4. nature _____
5. temperature _____
6. caution _____
7. direction _____
8. addition_____
9. attention _____
10. feature _____

11. ration _____
12. mature _____
13. pasture _____
14. texture _____
15. departure _____
16. mixture _____
17. section _____
18. notion _____
19. lecture _____
20. potion _____

Select three of the words above and write their definitions. Use a dictionary if needed.

21. _____
22. _____
23. _____

Have you ever been in a play or performance? What was it like? How often did you practice? What part did you play? On a separate sheet of paper, write about these questions. Underline the words that fit the rule.

Name _____   Date _____

Syllables (-ture, -tion)

Every word has at least one **syllable**. Each syllable must have a vowel sound. The vowel can be by itself or combined with one or more consonants.

Word	Syllables	Vowel Sounds	Number of Syllable
a	a	one vowel sound	one syllable
apple	ap/ple	two vowel sounds	two syllables
idea	i/de/a	three vowel sounds	three syllables

When *–ture* or *–tion* is at the end of a word, it forms its own syllable.

Example: na<u>tion</u>   na/tion

Read the paragraph. Underline the words that fit the rule.

Kenny works on a demolition crew. Each morning, Kenny reports to his station to get the day's directions. He has to pay careful attention so that he and his crew do not destroy the wrong building. One time, Kenny got the directions wrong and ended up at a pasture full of sheep! He was given a big lecture by the manager.

Divide each word into its syllables. Write each word only once.

1. _____   4. _____

2. _____   5. _____

3. _____   6. _____

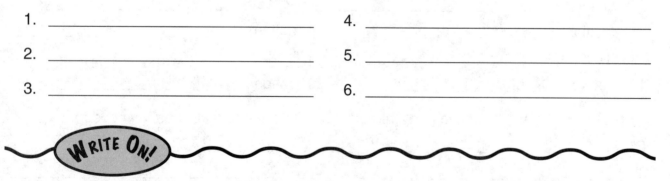

Have you ever misunderstood the directions you were given and done something that had an odd or unusual result? On a separate sheet of paper, write a paragraph telling about the experience.

Name _____ Date _____

Spelling Rules (q followed by u)

Spelling rules serve as a guide to spelling certain types of words. When spelling a word that uses a *q*, the *q* is always followed by a *u*.

Example: <u>qu</u>arter

Read the clues. Write a word from the Work Bank on the line.

Word Bank					
earthquake	equal	equipment	liquid	quarter	quarter
question	quickly	quiet	quill	quit	quit
quiz	racquet	request	sequel	queasy	queasy

1. To ask for information: _____

2. To not make a lot of noise: _____

3. To stop working at a job or task: _____

4. Teachers like to give this: _____

5. To politely ask for something: _____

6. To move fast: _____

7. Worth twenty-five cents: _____

8. Items for a sport: _____

9. Not a solid: _____

10. A second movie: _____

11. The pointy part of a porcupine: _____

12. Used to play tennis: _____

13. To have an upset stomach: _____

14. To be worth the same amount: _____

15. It shakes the ground: _____

WRITE ON!

On a separate sheet of paper, write a story using as many *qu* words as possible. Have a classmate read your story and underline each *qu* word.

Name _____ Date _____

Spelling Rules (q followed by u)

Spelling rules serve as a guide to spelling certain types of words. When spelling a word that uses a q, the q is always followed by a u.

Example: quarter

Read the paragraph. Underline any misspelled words. Write the correct spelling of the word above the line.

    Every qarter, our teacher likes to give us a pop qiz. The quiz has twenty questions on

everything that we have covered. The teacher has us place our desks an eqal distance

apart. Then she always gives us some kind of inspirational qote, the class gets qiet, and the

quiz begins. It is qickly over until the sequel next quarter!

Divide each now correctly spelled word into its syllables.

1. _____   3. _____   5 _____

2. _____   4. _____   6. _____

Write the definition for each word. Use a dictionary to look up any unfamiliar words.

7. quality: _____

8. quest: _____

9. marquee: _____

10. quip: _____

Think of a time you could not stop laughing. Where were you? What were you doing? What was so funny? On a separate sheet of paper, write the story and share it with a classmate. Try to use as many *qu* words as possible.

Name _____ Date _____

Spelling Rules (Silent e + Suffix)

Spelling rules serve as a guide to spelling certain types of words. If a word ends in silent *e*, drop the *e* before adding a suffix that begins with a vowel.

Example: ra<u>ge</u> + ing = raging

PRACTICE

Add the correct suffix to the word to complete each sentence.

–able   –age   –ing

Example: (hope) Elise is <u>hoping</u> that she will get a new bike for her birthday.

1. (*save*) Dean is _____ his money to buy a new car.

2. (*hide*) Benson is _____ under the bed.

3. (*live*) Was the home _____ after the fire and flood?

4. (*rake*) The kids are _____ the leaves.

5. (*drive*) The car was barely _____ after the accident.

6. (*like*) Ginger is a very _____ person.

7. (*tame*) The trainer is _____ the wild animal.

8. (*reuse*) Recycling means _____ things more than one time.

9. (*cure*) Is the disease _____ ?

10. (*bake*) Dad is _____ the cake for the party.

11. (*lace*) He finally is _____ his shoes by himself.

12. (*value*) Is the sunken treasure _____?

Write the base word.

13. leaving _____   17. paved _____

14. moveable _____   18. roughage _____

15. coming _____   19. moping _____

16. dining _____   20. striped _____

WRITE ON!

Where would you like to go to college? Why? On a separate sheet of paper, write a paragraph about this topic. Exchange papers with a classmate. Underline the words with silent *e* + a suffix.

Name _____   Date _____

Spelling Rules (Silent e + Suffix)

Spelling rules serve as a guide to spelling certain types of words. If a word ends in silent *e*, drop the *e* before adding a suffix that begins with a vowel.

Example: mak<u>e</u> + ing = making

Read the paragraph. Underline any misspelled words. Write the correct spelling of the word above the line.

    Mitchell loves bakeing during his free time. For the school bake sale, Mitchell was in his element. He spent the morning makying different kinds of cupcakes. Mitchell spent a lot of time decorateing the cupcakes useing sprinkles, frosting, and chocolate candies. After lunch, Mitchell made cookies. He made sugar cookies, peanut butter cookies, and chocolate chip cookies. All of the cookies were Mitchell's favorites!

Divide each now correctly spelled word into its syllables.

1. _____   3. _____

2. _____   4. _____

Write the definition for each word. Use a dictionary to look up any unfamiliar words.

5. salvage: _____

6. roughage: _____

7. scrambling: _____

8. sifting: _____

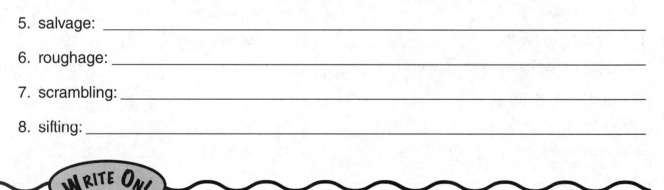

What kinds of items would you bake for a school bake sale? On a separate sheet of paper, write a paragraph about what you would make and why.

Name _____   Date _____

Spelling Rules (y + Suffix)

Spelling rules serve as a guide to spelling certain types of words. If a word <u>ends in consonant + y</u>, change the *y* to an *i* and add the suffix.

   Example: happy = happ<u>ily</u>

If a word <u>ends in vowel + y</u>, just add the suffix.

   Example: stay = stay<u>ed</u>

When <u>adding the suffix *–ing*</u>, keep the *y*. No change is needed.

   Example: study = study<u>ing</u>

PRACTICE

Add the correct suffix to the word to complete each sentence.

–ed	–ing	–ly

   Example: (*happy*) The group <u>happily</u> rowed down the stream.

1. (*study*) James _____ hard for the test.

2. (*lucky*) Teddy forgot his homework, but _____ his dad was able to bring it to school.

3. (*try*) Mother is _____ to find her missing car keys.

4. (*copy*) Sheila is always _____ someone else's work.

5. (*gray*) Grandpa's hair is rapidly _____.

6. (*stay*) Who is _____ at the cabin?

7. (*sloppy*) The room was _____ painted.

8. (*bury*) The dog _____ the bone in the backyard.

Read the paragraph. Underline any misspelled words. Write the correct spelling above the line.

   We are going to the local canyon. We are tring to get a bus that will hold all of our class, but we are haveing a difficult time. Last year, some of the kids staied behind because there wasn't enough room on the bus. We don't want that to happen again. Luckyily, one of the classmates' parents owns a large van and can take the extra kids!

WRITE ON!

On a separate sheet of paper, write about a favorite field trip. Where did you go? How did you get there? Underline any words that have a suffix.

Name _____ Date _____

Spelling Rules (y + Suffix)

Spelling rules serve as a guide to spelling certain types of words. If a word <u>ends in consonant + y</u>, change the *y* to an *i* and add the suffix.

Example: happy = happ<u>ily</u>

If a word <u>ends in vowel + y</u>, just add the suffix.

Example: stay = stay<u>ed</u>

When <u>adding the suffix *–ing*</u>, keep the *y*. No change is needed.

Example: study = stud<u>ying</u>

Read the paragraph. Underline any misspelled words. Write the correct spelling of the word above the line.

   I am studing to be a photographer like my Aunt Fran. She began takeing photographs at my age. She made her first camera useing an oatmeal box, tin foil, and photography paper. She shared with me her first photos, and they were really amazeing. Later, my aunt went to college and majored in photography. She took pictures for the school paper. After graduateing from college, my aunt worked for a local newspaper before she opened her own business. I am hopeing that I will be a great photographer like my aunt!

Divide each now correctly spelled word into its syllables.

1. _____ 3. _____ 5 _____

2. _____ 4. _____ 6. _____

Write the definition for each word. Use a dictionary to look up any unfamiliar words.

7. useful: _____

8. lovable: _____

9. princely: _____

10. adorable: _____

Think of a relative whose job you would like to have. What makes that job so interesting to you? Do you know how your relative first got started in that field? Use a separate sheet of paper to write a paragraph about this topic. Underline any words that have a suffix.

Vocabulary

Name _____ Date _____

Spelling Rules (Plural s and es)

Spelling rules serve as a guide to spelling certain types of words. To make a word plural (more than one), add an *s* to the end of the word.

   Example: lock = lock<u>s</u>

If the plural *s* sound is heard in the last syllable, then add *es* to the end of the word.

   Example: fox = fox<u>es</u>

Complete each sentence with the plural form of the word.

   Example: (*dress*) Mary has many <u>dresses</u>.

1. (*sandwich*) Jerry made one hundred peanut butter and jelly _____.

2. (*dot*) Karen loves to put _____ on everything.

3. (*truck*) The moving _____ came down the street.

4. (*shoulder*) The men put the heavy lumber on their _____.

5. (*tax*) Janet pays her _____ four times a year.

6. (*box*) How many _____ do you need?

7. (*sack*) Colin put the canned food into the paper _____.

8. (*mess*) Gracie made many _____ in the house.

9. (*stash*) Bea has many secret _____ for her money.

10. (*rash*) All of the campers came down with unusual _____.

11. (*eyelash*) Dwight has the longest _____.

12. (*crash*) Tarik was in ten _____ last year!

Write three words that fit each rule.

13. Add *s*: _____ , _____ , _____

14. Add *es*: _____ , _____ , _____

Have you ever had an accident while riding your bike or skateboard? What caused the accident? Were you hurt? On a separate sheet of paper, write a paragraph telling about the experience. Make sure you use words that contain the plural *s* or *es*. Underline them.

©*Teacher Created Resources, Inc.*   123   *#3993 Daily Warm-Ups: Language Skills*

Vocabulary

Name _____ Date _____

Spelling Rules (ie and ei)

Spelling rules serve as a guide to spelling certain types of words. Use *i* before *e* except after the *c*.

   Examples: bel<u>ie</u>ve, y<u>ie</u>ld, repr<u>ie</u>ve

Use *ei* if it follows the consonant *c*.

   Examples: c<u>ei</u>ling, perc<u>ei</u>ve, conc<u>ei</u>t

PRACTICE

Write the word that fits each riddle.

ceiling	
relieve	
yield	
niece	
shield	
chief	
field	
deceive	
believe	
fierce	
receive	
receipt	

1. _____: not the floor but overhead
2. _____: to slow down but not a complete stop
3. _____: worn by a police officer or held by a knight in shining armor
4. _____: where kids practice soccer
5. _____: what one thinks is true
6. _____: to get a phone call or mail
7. _____: a ticket showing what you paid for
8. _____: a strong, scary fighter
9. _____: to lie or cheat
10. _____: the head of the tribe, the boss
11. _____: not your nephew
12. _____: to give a break to

Read the paragraph. Underline any misspelled words. Write the word correctly above the line.

   We live in a really old house. Every time it rains, our ceeling leaks. It's like it is raining

right inside the house. We put out every pot and bucket that we have in order to sheeld the

carpets from the rain. But it doesn't help. By the time the rain is over, our carpet is like a

soggy football feeld. We will be releeved when we finally get the roof fixed!

WRITE ON!

On a separate sheet of paper, write about a favorite book. What makes the book so special to you? Use some *ie* or *ei* words and underline them.

Name _____ Date _____

Spelling Rules (ie and ei)

Spelling rules serve as a guide to spelling certain types of words. Use *i* before *e* except after the *c*.

Examples: bel<u>ie</u>ve, y<u>ie</u>ld, repr<u>ie</u>ve

Use *ei* if it follows the consonant *c*.

Examples: c<u>ei</u>ling, perc<u>ei</u>ve, conc<u>ei</u>t

If the *ei/ie* combination does not make the *ee* (long *e*) sound, then write *ei*, even if it doesn't follow the consonant *c*.

Examples: for<u>ei</u>gn, counterf<u>ei</u>t, r<u>ei</u>n

PRACTICE

Write the word that answers each definition.

1. _____ : person who lives next to you		neigh
2. _____ : worn by a bride to cover her face		veil
3. _____ : not native to the area		neighbor
4. _____ : a kind of train		veins
5. _____ : the number after seven		beige
6. _____ : what Santa drives		foreign
7. _____ : a person's length		leisure
8. _____ : step on a scale to find this		freight
9. _____ : pulls Santa's sleigh		reign
10. _____ : to rule over people		eight
11. _____ : one's free time		reindeer
12. _____ : they carry blood throughout your body		sleigh
13. _____ : a light brown color		weight
14. _____ : what a horse says		height

Write the group of words that rhyme from the list in the box.

_____ , _____ ,

_____

WRITE ON!

On a separate sheet of paper, write the rules for being a good neighbor. Share the rules with a classmate. Do they agree with your rules? Include *ie* and *ei* words.

Name _____   Date _____

Titles

Titles are the names of movies, books, songs, poems, and plays. All of the important words in the title are capitalized. The words *a, to, and, of,* and *the* are not capitalized unless they are the first word in the title. The title is also underlined for movies, books, and plays. The titles for songs and poems are set apart by quotation marks.

Examples:

   Movie title: Rudolph the Red-Nosed Reindeer

   Book title: Goldilocks and the Three Bears

   Song title: "We Wish You a Merry Christmas"

Correctly write a title for each category.

Favorite movie: _____

Favorite book: _____

Favorite song: _____

Favorite poem: _____

Favorite play: _____

Read the paragraph. Underline the titles in the paragraph.

   Last night, my grandpa and I went to see the latest play at the local theater. The play

The Lion and the Mouse was excellent! One of the actors had previously been in the action

movie Jump Off the High Cliff. The director had written a short book of poems called I Love

Trains. I was lucky enough to get both of their autographs.

On a separate sheet of paper, write a paragraph about a favorite movie, play, or book.
Remember to write the title correctly.

Name _____   Date _____

Titles

Titles are the names of movies, books, songs, poems, and plays. All of the important words in the title are capitalized. The words *a, to, and, of,* and *the* are not capitalized unless they are the first word in the title. The title is also underlined for movies, books, and plays. The titles for songs and poems are set apart by quotation marks.

Example: I saw the live performance of <u>Cinderella</u>.

Example: Have you ever read the poem, "Colors"?

PRACTICE

Rewrite each sentence correctly. Remember to capitalize the important words in the title and to underline or put quotes around the entire title.

Example: Who has seen the movie the carrot ate manhattan?
Who has seen the movie <u>The Carrot Ate Manhattan</u>?

1. i watched the street performance of a chocolate raindrop.

   _____

2. the song music for hippies is a number one hit!

   _____

3. for seventeen years, dogs! was a broadway hit!

   _____

4. at the end of the day is a very sad poem.

   _____

5. where is my dog? is the name of the play.

   _____

Read the paragraph. Underline the titles. Capitalize the important words in the title.

Last night, John and I went to see the hit movie my uncle is an alien. The movie was

extremely scary, but not as scary as your momma ate a train. The worst part of the movie

was when the uncle read part of the book garlic in my salad. John and I won't watch the

movie again!

WRITE ON!

On a separate sheet of paper, write a review about a movie that you saw. Remember to write the title of the movie correctly.

Mechanics and Usage

Name _____   Date _____

Quotation Marks

Quotation marks are used to show a person's exact spoken words. Capitalize the first word within the quotation marks. The ending punctuation mark is written before the final pair of quotation marks. Quotation marks are used to show exactly what Dad said.

Example: Dad said, "Let's go swimming."

Look at the example below. No quotation marks are used as Dad's exact words were not used.

Example: Dad said that we could go swimming.

PRACTICE

Rewrite only the sentences where someone's exact words were used. Add quotation marks around the person's words.

Example: I was invited to the movies, said Anna.

"I was invited to the movies," said Anna.

1. Where is my surfboard? asked Mavis.

   _____

2. Mavis was looking for her surfboard.

   _____

3. She has three teenage sons.

   _____

4. I have three teenage sons, said Nan.

   _____

5. I have a messy style, agreed Ryan.

   _____

6. Ryan agreed that his style was messy.

   _____

7. Sam found his sock behind his bed.

   _____

WRITE ON!

On a separate sheet of paper, write four sentences showing a person's exact words. Remember to use quotation marks around the person's words. Rewrite the same four sentences so that each sentence is not an exact quote of the person's words.

Name _____   Date _____

Quotation Marks

Quotation marks are used to show a person's exact spoken words. Capitalize the first word within the quotation marks. The ending punctuation mark is written before the final pair of quotation marks.

Example: Vincent cheered, "Hurray!"

Rewrite each sentence. Add quotation marks around the person's exact words. Capitalize the first word within the quotation marks. Include the ending punctuation mark before the final pair of quotation marks.

Example: Chris asked, where is the bench?

Chris asked, "Where is the bench?"

1. Walter said, i have three pets.

_____

2. my phone is ringing! exclaimed Marsha.

_____

3. my bunny's name is Smokey, Heidi said.

_____

4. Mark said, my last name is Smith.

_____

5. Grandpa asked, do you want to go to Maryland?

_____

6. Mom sighed, i love red cars.

_____

7. Sissy asked, who sat in my beanbag chair?

_____

Write a paragraph on a topic of your choice. Include one or two sentences where one of the characters says something. Remember to include quotations marks around the character's spoken words.

Name _____ Date _____

Quotation Marks

Quotation marks are used to show a person's exact spoken words. Capitalize the first word within the quotation marks. The ending punctuation mark is written before the final pair of quotation marks. Use a comma before the quotation marks.

Examples: Her sister said, "Lucy went jogging."

Mrs. Nash said, "Today is cleaning day!"

Paul asked, "Who won the race?"

PRACTICE

Rewrite each sentence correctly using quotation marks and ending punctuation.

Example: James said, the beach is a great place to visit.

James said, "The beach is a great place to visit!"

1. Paul ran down the street screaming, I saw a hamster!

   _____

2. Dr. Taylor said, Eat an apple every day.

   _____

3. Mom asked, Did you write it on the calendar?

   _____

4. Grandma said, I made the wooden train.

   _____

5. Linda asked, Who made this mess?

   _____

6. Jeff and Brandon both shouted, Hurray!

   _____

Write two sentences showing a person's exact words. Remember to correctly use quotation marks and ending punctuation.

_____

_____

WRITE ON!

On a separate sheet of paper, write about a time that you were surprised by something. Use quotation marks to show your spoken words. Share the paragraph with a classmate.

Name _____   Date _____

Quotation Marks

Quotation marks are used to show a person's exact spoken words. Capitalize the first word within the quotation marks. The ending punctuation mark is written before the final pair of quotation marks.

Use a comma before (or after) the quotation marks. The comma follows the speaker (Maria said,) or comes after the final word in the quote (, said Maria.). Look at the examples below.

Brandon asked, "Where is the remote control?"

Mom said, "I don't know. Did you check under the couch?"

"Ummm, Brandon, you might want to check in your pocket," said Mom.

"Oh," said Brandon.

Rewrite the text correctly using quotation marks and ending punctuation.

Uncle Joe came to spend the day with us. Uncle Joe asked, What would you two chaps like to do today?

I said, Let's go to the park and play soccer!

My little brother said, No! I want to go rollerblading.

Uncle Joe laughed and said I know what we will do. We'll play soccer before lunch and go rollerblading after lunch!

My little brother and I said, Great idea, Uncle Joe!

_____

_____

_____

_____

_____

_____

_____

_____

On a separate sheet of paper, write a paragraph about when you and your family had to decide on an activity. Use quotation marks to show what each person said.

Name _____ Date _____

Quotation Marks

Quotation marks are used to show a person's exact spoken words. Capitalize the first word within the quotation marks. The ending punctuation mark is written before the final pair of quotation marks.

Use a comma before (or after) the quotation marks. The comma follows the speaker (Maria said,) or comes after the final word in the quote (, said Maria.).

Each time a new person speaks, start a new paragraph. Look at the example below.

Bea asked, "When is dinner?"

Dad said, "Dinner will be ready in a few minutes. Why don't you eat a celery stick if you are hungry?"

Bea said, "That's a good idea, Dad. I'm so hungry I could eat a horse!"

Rewrite the dialogue. Remember to begin a new paragraph for each new speaker.

Where is the dog? asked Robert. I can't find her and I've looked everywhere! Have you checked outside? asked Ruby. Yes, I even looked in her doghouse, replied Robert. Well, maybe she's out in the garage, suggested Ruby. Good thinking, Ruby. I will check there next, said Robert.

_____

_____

_____

_____

_____

_____

_____

_____

On a separate sheet of paper, write about a time that you lost something and what you did to find it. Remember to indent for each new speaker and to use quotation marks around the speaker's exact words. Share the story with a classmate.

Name _____ Date _____

Colons

A **colon** is made with two dots. A colon looks like this **(:)**. Use a colon to separate an independent clause from an explanation or list. (An independent clause can stand by itself as a complete sentence.)

Example: My wheelchair has many parts: wheels, back, joystick, basket, and armrests.

The independent clause is "My wheelchair has many parts." This is a complete sentence.

Read the underlined part in each sentence. If the underline part is an independent clause, circle the entire sentence.

Example: (Sal is great at fixing many things: plumbing, wiring and flooring.)

1. Wolves can be found in many different stories: "Little Red Riding Hood," "The Three Little Pigs," and "The Gingerbread Man."

2. When I am packing my suitcase, I always include plenty of socks.

3. Brittle bones have many causes: poor diet, lack of calcium, and heredity.

4. Being tall is not a picnic: being short is not a picnic, either.

5. Be proud of yourself: you did a great job!

6. When I am happy, I sing, dance, and twirl around.

7. Plants need three things to grow: sunlight, water, and soil.

8. I like two kinds of cars: fast and faster.

9. I visited many cities this summer: San Francisco, Los Angeles, Bakersfield, Visalia, and Clovis.

10. At the mini mart, I bought a slush drink, a candy bar, and a pack of gum.

On a separate sheet of paper, write on a topic of your choice. Be sure to include an independent clause (a sentence that can stand by itself) followed by a list of items or an explanation.

Mechanics and Usage

Name _____   Date _____

Colons

A **colon** is made with two dots. A colon looks like this (**:**). Use a colon to separate an independent clause from an explanation or list. (An independent clause can stand by itself as a complete sentence.) A comma is used after each item.

Example: I packed many items in my suitcase: pants, shirts, socks, shoes, and belts.

For each topic, write an independent clause followed by a list of items.

Example: (fruit) I bought many different kinds of fruit at the fruit stand: strawberries, apples, bananas, and oranges.

1. (zoo animals) _____

   _____

2. (desserts) _____

   _____

3. (plants) _____

   _____

4. (school supplies) _____

   _____

5. (colors) _____

   _____

6. (pant sizes) _____

   _____

7. (diseases) _____

   _____

8. (sea animals) _____

   _____

On separate sheet of paper, write a paragraph on a topic of your choice. Be sure to include an independent clause followed by a list of items.

Mechanics and Usage

Name _____   Date _____

Colons

A **colon** is made with two dots. A colon looks like this (**:**).
Use a colon after a *formal* greeting when writing a letter.

  Example: Dear Sir:

Use a comma after an *informal* greeting when writing a
friendly letter to someone you know.

  Example: Hi Fred,

PRACTICE

Decide if the greeting is *formal* or *informal* and then write the type of punctuation needed.

  Example: To Whom It May Concern   <u>formal</u>   <u>colon</u>

  1. Dear President Jones   _____   _____

  2. Dear Mom   _____   _____

  3. Hola Sammy   _____   _____

  4. Dear Madam   _____   _____

  5. Dear Sir   _____   _____

  6. Hi Jessica   _____   _____

  7. Hello Annie   _____   _____

  8. Dear Principal Adams   _____   _____

  9. My Dearest Granny   _____   _____

  10. Dear Son   _____   _____

WRITE ON!

On a separate sheet of paper, write a formal letter. Remember to use a colon after the greeting.
Send or give the letter to the appropriate person.

Name _____   Date _____

Colons

A **colon** is made with two dots. A colon looks like this (:). A colon is used to separate a word from its definition. Look at the example below.

stature: a person's height or standing in the community

Use a colon to separate the word from its meaning. Look at the example below.

necklace: a piece of jewelry worn around the neck

1. hair   furry covering on the body or head

2. umbrella   used to cover oneself when it is raining

3. box   a container with six sides

4. belt   an article of clothing worn around the waist

5. stripes   vertical or horizontal lines

Write a definition for each word. If you are not sure what the word means, look it up in a dictionary. Remember to use a colon to separate the word from its meaning.

6. shoe _____

7. marker _____

8. paper _____

9. camera _____

10. bowling _____

Read the story. Add a colon where needed.

    I made sure the dogs had everything they needed: food, water, bowls, and toys. Then I put the dogs into the car and drove them to Grandma's house. Grandma said to put the dogs in the kennel. I didn't know what a kennel was. I looked in a dog book. It said, "kennel a cage for dogs." I put the dogs and their items in the kennel.

On a separate sheet of paper, make a list of words that you do not know. Use the dictionary to help you. Make sure to list the word and its meaning. Don't forget to use a colon.

Name _____   Date _____

Ending Punctuation

Every sentence begins with a capital letter and ends with a period, question mark, or exclamation point.

Use a **period (.)** at the end of a statement (telling) sentence or command (order).

   Examples: I missed the bus. (*statement*)

                Don't miss the bus. (*command*)

Identify each sentence as a *statement* or a *command*.

   Example: Wash the dirty dishes.   <u> command </u>

  1. I can sharpen the pencils. _____

  2. I don't know. _____

  3. Go put on your shoes. _____

  4. Collectible dolls can be worth a lot of money. _____

  5. Michael has a new scooter. _____

  6. I rode it two months ago. _____

  7. The lemon trees are growing well. _____

  8. Shut the door. _____

  9. I will go to the party. _____

 10. Pour the batter into the pans. _____

Rewrite each statement as a command.

  Example: Kwan hangs up his clothes.   <u>Hang up the clothes</u>.

 11. The students will not talk in the library. _____

 12. All cars will stop at the sign. _____

Rewrite each command as a statement.

  Example: No skateboarding on the sidewalk.   <u>Mark will not skateboard on the sidewalk</u>.

 13. Go home. _____

 14. Sweep the sidewalk. _____

On a separate sheet of paper, write a paragraph using both commands and statements. Have a classmate circle the command sentences and underline the statements.

Name _____   Date _____

Ending Punctuation

Every sentence begins with a capital letter and ends with a period, question mark, or exclamation point.

Use a **period (.)** at the end of a statement (telling) sentence or command (order).
   Examples: My neighbor jogs every morning. (*statement*)
                Exercise every day. (*command*)

Write five statements.

  1. _____
  2. _____
  3. _____
  4. _____
  5. _____

Write five commands.

  6. _____
  7. _____
  8. _____
  9. _____
10. _____

Read the paragraph. Circle the command sentences. Underline the statements.

    Henry's dad was helping him make a kite. "Get two sticks and tie them together," said Dad. Henry got two sticks and used twine to tie them together.

    "Now," said Dad, "tie a piece of string so that it goes around the outside of the sticks."

    "Okay," said Henry. Henry tied the string so that it touched the end of each stick.

    "We can put the large paper over the frame and glue it around the string," said Dad. Henry and Dad glued the paper to the frame and were ready to fly the kite!

On a separate sheet of paper, write a paragraph about doing a certain task. Be sure to include both statements and command sentences in the paragraph.

Name _____ Date _____

Ending Punctuation

Every sentence begins with a capital letter and ends with a period, question mark, or exclamation point.

Use a **question mark (?)** at the end of an interrogatory (asking) sentence.

   Example: Do you have lunch money? (*question*)

             I have lunch money. (*statement*)

PRACTICE

Underline the sentences that are questions and then add the appropriate ending punctuation to those sentences.

  1. Do you want to go to the store

  2. I went to the store

  3. Where is Matilda

  4. Matilda is outside

  5. Let's go to the mountains

  6. Have you ever been to the mountains

  7. What is peach fuzz

  8. Peach fuzz is the furry skin covering a peach

  9. Do you have a big family

 10. I have a small family

Write two questions. Remember to begin each sentence with a capital letter and end the sentence with a question mark.

 11. _____

 12. _____

WRITE ON!

On a separate sheet of paper, write a paragraph about a new interest. In the paragraph, ask a question about the topic. Share the paragraph with a classmate.

Name _____ Date _____

Ending Punctuation

Every sentence begins with a capital letter and ends with a period, question mark, or exclamation point.

Use a **question mark (?)** at the end of an interrogatory (asking) sentence.

   Example: Did you see the eclipse?

Write an interrogatory sentence for each topic.

   Example: world: <u>How many people live in the world?</u>

   1. furniture: _____

   2. computer: _____

   3. table: _____

   4. cane: _____

   5. chair: _____

   6. throw: _____

   7. plant: _____

   8. push: _____

   9. television: _____

  10. bench: _____

Read the paragraph. Circle the interrogatory sentences.

   Last night, my friends and I decided to watch a scary movie.

   Mom asked, "Are you sure that's a good idea? You know how scary movies give you nightmares."

   I said, "Don't be silly, Mom. We are big now. We are not little kids." My friends and I watched *The Zombie that Attacked Manhattan*.

   Marcie asked, "Is anybody else getting scared?"

   I said, "I'm not scared! Are you?"

   Betsy said, "I'm getting a little bit scared. Maybe we should watch something else. What do you think?"

On a separate sheet of paper, write a paragraph about meeting someone new. What would you say to the person? What questions would you ask? What would you tell the person about yourself?

Name _____ Date _____

Ending Punctuation

Every sentence begins with a capital letter and ends with a period, question mark, or exclamation point.

Use an **exclamation point (!)** to show strong emotion: surprise, anger, excitement, joy, sadness, or happiness.

Example: That is the ugliest tie I've ever seen!

Read each pair of sentences. Circle the sentence that should have an exclamation point at the end.

1. Richard was running in the marathon. He won with the fastest time ever.
2. Jerome made the most delicious cake. It was chocolate with buttercream frosting.
3. I love that design. Circles are my favorite shape.
4. That music is so loud. Maybe they should turn it down.
5. There's Fido. We had been looking for him all day.
6. The fire engine roared by. The fire engine was going to the largest fire ever.
7. Be careful. There is broken glass everywhere.
8. Don't look directly at the sun. It will burn your eyes.
9. Your hair is so long. It is just like your mom's.
10. I went to get on my bike. All of the tires were flat.

Write an exclamatory sentence about each topic.

11. Losing a game

    _____

12. Taking first place in the spelling bee

    _____

13. Crashing a car

    _____

14. Finding a million dollars

    _____

15. Being in a parade

    _____

On a separate sheet of paper, write a paragraph about an exciting event. Remember to use exclamation points at the end of sentences that show strong emotion.

Name _____   Date _____

Ending Punctuation

Every sentence begins with a capital letter and ends with a period, question mark, or exclamation point.

Use an **exclamation point** (!) to show strong emotion: surprise, anger, excitement, joy, sadness, or happiness.

   Example: What a disaster!

Read the paragraph. Circle the sentences that should have exclamation points at the end.

   Jerry was skateboarding down the sidewalk. He stopped at the corner and waited until it was safe to cross the street. As Jerry crossed the street, a large semitruck came barreling down the street. Jerry quickly jumped back onto the sidewalk. He was almost hit by the semitruck. His skateboard wasn't so lucky. It was smashed to smithereens.

Rewrite the paragraph using correct ending punctuation.

_____

_____

_____

_____

_____

_____

_____

_____

_____

_____

_____

On a separate sheet of paper, write a paragraph about something exciting that happened to you. Remember to use appropriate ending punctuation.

Name _____ Date _____

Periods in Abbreviations

A **period** is used to signal the end of a statement or a command. A period is also used in writing abbreviations. Abbreviations are a shorter way of writing a longer word.

   Example: Mister = Mr.

When the abbreviation ends the sentence, do not use another period to mark the end of the sentence.

   Example: Mark lives in Washington, D.C.

The abbreviations for proper nouns begin with a capital letter.

   Example: Mooney Boulevard = Mooney Blvd.

Write the abbreviation for each word.

1. Mister _____
2. yard _____
3. Junior _____
4. Captain _____
5. Lane _____

6. Avenue _____
7. Mistress _____
8. mile _____
9. feet _____
10. Sergeant _____

11. Senior _____
12. Doctor _____
13. Street _____
14. Saint _____
15. inch _____

Underline the abbreviations used in the paragraph. Rewrite the paragraph spelling out the abbreviations.

   Last weekend, my family and I went camping at Mt. Shasta. We pitched our tents at the campground. The tents were about three ft. apart. We then walked about half a mi. down the path to Lake Full-of-Water. We caught many fish. We walked back up Mulberry Rd. and spread the fish out over two yd. of clothesline. We built a fire under the clothesline about six in. under the fish. Capt. White came by to make sure we were following the local fire rules. We had a great time camping!

On a separate sheet of paper, write about a good time you had with your family or friends. What did you do? Did you go somewhere? Be sure to include some abbreviations in your story. Exchange papers with a classmate. Have the classmate circle all of the abbreviations used in the story and write out the abbreviations at the bottom of the page. Did your classmate catch all of the abbreviations? Did your classmate correctly spell out each abbreviation?

Name _____ Date _____

Periods in Abbreviations

A **period** is used to signal the end of a statement or a command. A period is also used in writing abbreviations. Abbreviations are a shorter way of writing a longer word.

  Example: Mister = Mr.

When the abbreviation ends the sentence, do not use another period to mark the end of the sentence. But do use the question mark or exclamation point, if appropriate for the sentence.

  Example: Have you ever been to L.A.?

The abbreviations for proper nouns begin with a capital letter.

  Example: Serena Avenue = Serena Ave.

Underline the abbreviation used in each sentence. Spell out the abbreviation on the line.

  Example: <u>Det.</u> Malone solved the crime!   <u>Detective</u>

1. Mr. Douglas enjoys gardening. _____

2. Stan Sr. is on a diet. _____

3. Where is Jr.? _____

4. Dr. Leon takes care of many of the children in town. _____

5. Make a left on Lester Blvd. _____

6. Erica's birthday is on Dec. 23. _____

7. Mon. is the first school day of each week. _____

8. St. Patrick's Day is March 17. _____

9. Who has a house on Rd. 180? _____

10. First, take Hwy. 41 north to Coarsegold. _____

Use each abbreviation in a sentence.

11. Sgt. _____

12. Jr. _____

13. ft. _____

14. mi. _____

On a separate sheet of paper, write the directions to get to your favorite place. Use abbreviations for the streets or roads that are used. Exchange papers with a classmate. Have the classmate circle the abbreviations and write out the abbreviations at the bottom of the page.

Mechanics and Usage

Name _____ Date _____

Periods in Abbreviations

A **period** is used to signal the end of a statement or a command. A period is also used in writing abbreviations. Abbreviations are a shorter way of writing a longer word.

Example: Abbreviation = abbrev.

To write the abbreviations for the days of the week and the months of the year, write the first three letters of the name followed by a period.

Examples: January = Jan.   Saturday = Sat.

Remember to capitalize the first letter of each abbreviation as the names of each day and each month are proper nouns.

PRACTICE

Write the abbreviation for the following days of the week and months of the year.

1. Monday_____   4. Tuesday_____   7. Thursday_____

2. March _____   5. April _____   8. May_____

3. December_____   6. Friday _____   9. August _____

Underline the name of the week or the month of the year used in each sentence. Write the abbreviation for each word on the line.

Example: My birthday is in <u>March</u>.   _____ Mar. _____

10. When will it be Saturday?   _____

11. How many birthdays are in January?   _____

12. My parents' anniversary is in November.   _____

13. Wednesday is the fourth day of the week.   _____

14. Valentine's Day is in February.   _____

15. Which month comes after October?   _____

16. Field Day will be held on Friday.   _____

17. Sunday is a day of rest.   _____

18. School starts in September.   _____

19. Is December the last month of the year?   _____

WRITE ON!

On a separate sheet of paper, write a paragraph about a special event. Make sure to include when the event occurs. Underline all of the words that could be abbreviated. Write the abbreviations at the bottom of the page.

Name _____   Date _____

Periods in Abbreviations

A **period** is used to signal the end of a statement or a command. A period is also used in writing abbreviations. Abbreviations are a shorter way of writing a longer word.

Example: Street = St.

When writing the abbreviations for the different states, use two capital letters and no periods. For most states, the abbreviation is made using the first two letters in the state's name.

Example: Alabama = AL

For states with two names, the abbreviation is made using the first letter from each part of the state's name.

Example: North Carolina = NC

PRACTICE

Underline the name of each state. Write the state's abbreviation on the line.

Example: <u>Rhode Island</u> is a small state.   _____ RI

1. Former President Clinton is from Arkansas.   _____

2. Florida is known for producing great oranges.   _____

3. "The Big Apple" is a nickname for a city in New York.   _____

4. Have you ever been to West Virginia?   _____

5. I think South Carolina is on the east coast.   _____

6. I have been skiing in Colorado.   _____

7. Potatoes are grown in Idaho.   _____

8. The Boston Tea Party occurred in Boston, Massachusetts.   _____

9. My brother was named after North Dakota.   _____

10. Rachel went horseback riding in Wyoming.   _____

Write the abbreviations for the following states.

11. California _____   15. Nebraska _____   19. Indiana _____

12. Delaware _____   16. South Dakota _____   20. Utah _____

13. Ohio _____   17. North Carolina _____   21. Wisconsin _____

14. Oregon _____   18. New Jersey _____   22. New Mexico _____

WRITE ON!

On a separate sheet of paper, write a paragraph about the states that you have visited. Circle the names of the states and write their abbreviations at the bottom of the page.

Name _____   Date _____

Commas

Use a **comma (,)** to separate items in a list or to separate a series of phrases.

Example: Joe bought a monkey wrench, a screwdriver, a pair of pliers, and a hammer.

Rewrite each sentence using commas as needed.

Example: Today I worked in the yard cleaned the kitchen and washed the windows.
Today, I worked in the yard, cleaned the kitchen, and washed the windows.

1. The bicycle has a basket a horn a seat and a headlight.
   _____

2. Mike plays baseball football hockey and basketball.
   _____

3. To plant a seed, dig a hole put the seed in cover the seed with soil and water the seed.
   _____

4. Have you seen Millie Molly or Melly?
   _____

5. Do you want pumpkin apple or cherry pie?
   _____

6. The president vice-president secretary and chairperson attended the fundraiser.
   _____

7. The elephant eats peanuts hay grass and apples.
   _____

8. The baby cries kicks coos chortles and sighs.
   _____

9. Do you know how to play the piano flute organ or trumpet?
   _____

10. Aunt Sally planted peach trees apple trees orange trees and cherry trees.
    _____

Write a paragraph about making your favorite after-school snack. What items do you need?
How do you go about making the snack? Remember to use commas to separate the items in a
list or a series of phrases.

Name _____   Date _____

Commas

Use a **comma (,)** before a conjunction. Conjunctions are *for, and, nor, but, or, yet, so.*
   Example: The singer was great, <u>so</u> we stayed to hear her encore performance.

Underline the conjunction. Then add a comma before each conjunction.

   Example: Joy likes to watch scary movies, <u>but</u> they give her nightmares.

1. I don't know where the laundry chute is but I do know where the trash chute is.

2. I like chocolate and I like vanilla.

3. Margo was sick so she missed the test.

4. My sister likes the attention yet the rest of the family doesn't.

5 Do you want to take the stairs or do you prefer to take the elevator?

6. Ava can have the boogie board or she can have the sand toys.

7. Jordan built a fire and he cooked the fish.

8. Lori does not have her cell phone nor does she have a quarter to make a phone call.

9. The car broke down yet everyone arrived on time.

10. Anna takes gymnastics so she is very flexible.

Add commas to the paragraph.

   Angelina wants to be a clothes designer yet she does not sew very well. She has been

taking sewing lessons for many years but she still does not know how to sew on a button.

Angelina hopes one day to learn how but for now she just asks her mom to help her with

sewing.

On a separate sheet of paper, write a paragraph about something you enjoy doing, but cannot
do very well. Remember to use a comma before any conjunctions.

Name _____ Date _____

Commas

Use a **comma (,)** after introductory clauses.

   Examples: While we were waiting, we watched the movie.

Introductory clauses begin with the following:

after	although	as	because
if	since	when	while

PRACTICE

Finish each sentence. Remember to use a comma after each introductory clause.

1. After _____
  _____.

2. Although I like _____
  _____.

3. As I mentioned _____
  _____.

4. Because _____
  _____.

5. If you _____
  _____.

6. Since he was _____
  _____.

7. When are _____
  _____.

8. While _____
  _____.

Read the paragraph. Add a comma after each introductory clause.

   Since Mom said that we could get a pet we all went to the pet store. While we were looking at the rabbits I saw the cutest puppy! He was so lively and had huge paws. When Mom saw the puppy she agreed he was cute. Although we had planned on getting a rabbit we ended up taking home a puppy!

WRITE ON!

Have you ever gone to the shopping mall to get one thing and came home with something completely different? On a separate sheet of paper, write a paragraph about the experience. Remember to use a comma after any introductory clauses.

Name _____ Date _____

Commas

Use a **comma (,)** when writing dates. The comma separates the day and the year.
  Example: January 21, 2007.

Use a comma when writing the city and its state. The comma separates the city from the state.
  Examples: Clovis, California
       Clovis, CA
       Clovis, California, is located in the Central Valley.

Use a comma when writing out an address. The comma separates the street name from the city and state.
  Examples: 123 Main Street, Fresno, California
       123 Main Street, Fresno, CA
       Jane and Harry Smith, 123 Main Street, Fresno, California

PRACTICE

Write the following information.

  1. Write today's date. _____

  2. Write your birthday. _____

  3. Write the date of your favorite holiday. _____

  4. Write the name of the city and state you live in. _____

  5. Write a sentence using the name of your city and state.

     _____

  6. Write your complete address.

     _____

Read the paragraph. Use a caret (∧) to insert any missing commas.

    Last month on July 15 2007 my family and I went to visit our relatives in Cincinnati Ohio.

  Our relatives live in a two-story house at 3540 Sycamore Street. Our relatives Aunt Sue and

  Uncle Billy have five kids. The kids' names are Pat Larry Joe Darlene and Opal. Our cousins

  are in third grade fourth grade fifth grade sixth grade and seventh grade.

WRITE ON!

On a separate sheet of paper, write about a time that you went to visit a relative, even if you just went next door! When did you go? Whom did you visit? What was the address of your relative's house? Remember to include commas when writing dates, addresses, and lists of names!

Name _____   Date _____

Apostrophes

An **apostrophe** (') is used to make a noun possessive. A possessive noun shows ownership.

Example: That computer belongs to Warren.

That is Warren's computer.

Change each sentence to a phrase that shows ownership.

Example: The sticks belong to the little pig.   The little pig's sticks

1. The jacket belongs to Nancy. _____

2. The sweater is owned by the Chihuahua. _____

3. The report card belongs to Susie. _____

4. The work was done by Frankie. _____

5. The computer is owned by Wendy. _____

Write a sentence to show ownership.

Example: headlights, car   The car's headlights were turned on high beam.

6. sneakers, Charlie

_____

7. blanket, Billy

_____

8. stapler, Mr. Smitty

_____

9. volleyball, the team

_____

10. apple, Fritz

_____

On a separate sheet of paper, write about a favorite item. What makes the item so special to you? What do you do with the item? Where do you keep it? What does it look like? Share the paragraph with a classmate.

Name _____ Date _____

Apostrophes

An **apostrophe** (') is used when writing contractions. A contraction is made by combining two words into one shorter word. The apostrophe takes the place of the missing letter or letters.

Example: would not = wouldn't

The apostrophe takes the place of the missing *o* in *not*.

Write the contraction for each word.

1. we are _____
2. are not _____
3. he is _____
4. do not _____

5. it is _____
6. they would _____
7. she will _____
8. does not _____

9. will not _____
10. they are _____
11. I am _____
12. you are _____

Rewrite each sentence using contractions.

13. We are not going to be late for the train.

_____

14. He is getting another parking ticket!

_____

15. Do not drive on the wrong side of the road.

_____

16. I am first in line.

_____

17. They are moving to a new city.

_____

18. This plan will not work.

_____

19. This does not sound like a good idea to me.

_____

20. She will work hard at her new job.

_____

On a separate sheet of paper, tell about your favorite flavor of ice cream. What is your favorite way to eat it? Rewrite your paragraph using contractions to replace pairs of words when possible.

Name _____   Date _____

Dictionary Skills

Dictionary skills are needed in order to use a dictionary efficiently. For each word, a dictionary provides the following:

- The meanings (definitions) for the word
- The part (or parts) of speech
- A pronunciation
- Example sentences or phrases using the word

In order to use a dictionary effectively, you need to know how to alphabetize words.

Example: kitchen, cutlery, cabinet

Alphabetical order: cabinet, cutlery, kitchen

For each set of words, write the one that would be first alphabetically on the line.

Example: garden, grass, plant   _garden_

1. rake, wheelbarrow, hoe   _____

2. dirt, tree, sapling   _____

3. plants, seed, soil   _____

4. stake, vine, twine   _____

5. bush, shrub, flower   _____

6. shovel, trowel, broom   _____

Write a definition for each word you wrote on the line. Compare your definitions to those a classmate wrote. Are the definitions similar?

7. _____

8. _____

9. _____

10. _____

11. _____

12. _____

Besides looking up words, for what else could you use a dictionary? Pretend you are trying to sell dictionaries to a friend. Tell your friend what is so great about them. Write your answer on a separate sheet of paper.

Name _____   Date _____

Dictionary Skills

Dictionary skills are needed in order to use a dictionary efficiently. For each word, a dictionary provides the following:

- The meanings (definitions) for the word
- The part (or parts) of speech
- A pronunciation
- Example sentences or phrases using the word

In order to use a dictionary effectively, you need to know how to alphabetize words.

   Example: lumber, crate, dolly

            Alphabetical order: crate, dolly, lumber

PRACTICE

Write the words in alphabetical order.

sofa	1.	_____
chair	2.	_____
fireplace	3.	_____
mirror	4.	_____
picture	5.	_____
clock	6.	_____
book	7.	_____
television	8.	_____
carpet	9.	_____
window	10.	_____

Pick one of the words from the list. Use the word in each of the following types of sentences.

11. Command: _____

12. Statement: _____

13. Interrogatory: _____

14. Exclamatory: _____

WRITE ON!

On a separate sheet of paper, write how you have used a dictionary. How did you find the word you were looking for? What did the dictionary look like? Underline ten words from your story. Have a classmate write the words in alphabetical order.

Name _____ Date _____

Dictionary Skills

Dictionary skills are needed in order to use a dictionary efficiently. For each word, a dictionary provides the following:

- The meanings (definitions) for the word
- The part (or parts) of speech
- Example sentences or phrases using the word
- A pronunciation

At the top of each page in a dictionary, there are two *guide words*. The guide words let you know what the first word is on the page and what the last word is on the page.

blanket   47   chest

Any words that come alphabetically between the two guide words will be found on this page.

PRACTICE

Answer the questions below using the guide words found above in the book above.

Word List							
cider	dresser	checkers	cinder	cat	cast	castle	baby
alligator	brunch	chicken	brick	deer	can	cup	donut
bland	calculator	breakfast	design	buy	paper	duck	bump

1. What are the two guide words on the page in the book? _____

2. What is the first word with a definition on this page? _____

3. What is the last word with a definition on this page? _____

4. Look at the list of words. Write the words that would be found on this page.

_____

_____

_____

WRITE ON!

Pretend you are a dictionary. What would you have to say to people? On a separate sheet of paper, write a paragraph about life from the point of view of a dictionary. Share your paragraph with a classmate.

Name _____   Date _____

Dictionary Skills

Dictionary skills are needed in order to use a dictionary efficiently. For each word, a dictionary provides the following:

- The meanings (definitions) for the word
- The part (or parts) of speech
- A pronunciation
- Example sentences or phrases using the word

At the top of each page in a dictionary, there are two *guide words*. The guide words let you know what the first word is on the page and what the last word is on the page.

Any words that come alphabetically between the two guide words will be found on this page.

Write the following words on the correct page in the dictionary below. (*Note*: Not all of the words will be used! To make this task easier, alphabetize the words on a separate sheet of paper. Then write the words on the correct dictionary page.)

belt	best	bed	breath	bell	break	brew	bead
brand	button	better	blend	breathe	bottom	beak	bet
bend	brain	bark	brake	bland	beard	bran	bled

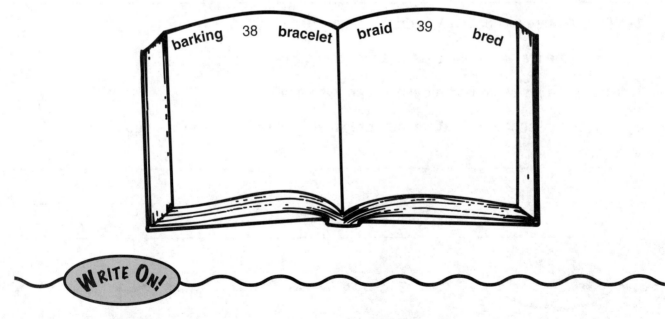

Pretend you dropped the dictionary and all of the words in the dictionary became scrambled! What would you do? How would you find the word that you needed? On a separate sheet of paper, write your answer to this situation.

Name _____ Date _____

Dictionary Skills

Dictionary skills are needed in order to use a dictionary efficiently. For each word, a dictionary provides the following:

- The meanings (definitions) for the word
- The part (or parts) of speech
- A pronunciation
- Example sentences or phrases using the word

At the top of each page in a dictionary, there are two *guide words*. The guide words let you know what the first word is on the page and what the last word is on the page.

Any words that come alphabetically between the two guide words will be found on this page.

PRACTICE

Write the following words on the correct page in the dictionary. (*Note:* Not all of the words will be used! To make this task easier, alphabetize the words on a separate sheet of paper. Then write the words on the correct dictionary page.)

dug	fun	ear	gum	eel	did	fruit	eat
dinghy	go	eagle	dandy	fancy	elephant	goes	fill
each	debt	fat	east	gumbo	farm	din	field

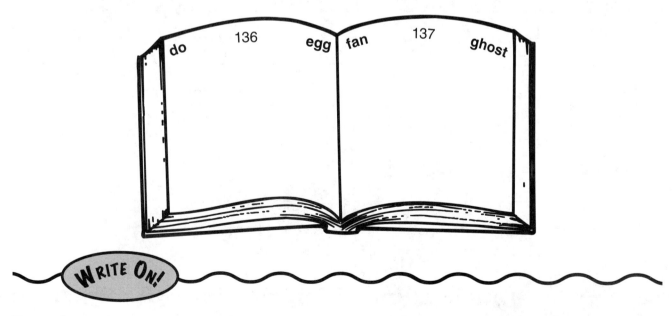

WRITE ON!

Pretend you are a word detective. You need to find out the meaning of a word without looking it up in a dictionary. How are you going to solve this mystery? On a separate sheet of paper, write your answer.

Name _____   Date _____

Dictionary Skills

Dictionary skills are needed in order to use a dictionary efficiently. For each word, a dictionary provides the following:

- The meanings (definitions) for the word
- The part (or parts) of speech
- A pronunciation
- Example sentences or phrases using the word

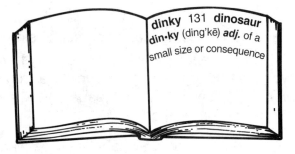

At the top of each page in a dictionary, there are two *guide words*. The guide words let you know what the first word is on the page and what the last word is on the page.

Example: dinky–dinosaur

An *entry word* is one of the words found on any page in the dictionary.

Example: **din·ky** (ding´kē) **adj.** of a small size or consequence

PRACTICE

Use a dictionary to find the following information about each word.

Example:

Entry Word	Pronunciation	Part of Speech	Meaning
tad·pole	(tad´pol´)	noun	The larval stage of a frog or toad
1. pup·py	_____	_____	_____
2. gos·ling	_____	_____	_____
3. duck·ling	_____	_____	_____
4. colt	_____	_____	_____
5. kit·ten	_____	_____	_____
6. calf	_____	_____	_____

Add five more words that would fit this list.

7. _____   10. _____

8. _____   11. _____

9. _____

WRITE ON!

On a separate sheet of paper, write a paragraph about an animal. Write all the facts you know about that animal. Share the paragraph with a classmate.

Name _____ Date _____

Dictionary Skills

Dictionary skills are needed in order to use a dictionary efficiently. For each word, a dictionary provides the following:

- The meanings (definitions) for the word
- The part (or parts) of speech
- A pronunciation
- Example sentences or phrases using the word

At to the top of each page in a dictionary, there are two *guide words.* The guide words tell what the first word is on the page and what the last word is on the page.

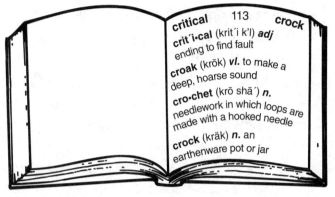

Example: critical–crock

An entry word is one of the words found on any page in the dictionary. For example, if a dictionary page had the guide words *critica*l and *crock*, the entry word below might be found on that page.

Entry word: **croak** (krōk) *n.* (noun) to make a deep, hoarse sound

PRACTICE

Open a dictionary to any page. Find the following information.

1. Page number: _____

2. Guide words: _____

3. Total number of entry words on the page: _____

Find the following information for six entry words on that particular page.

Entry Word	Pronunciation	Part of Speech	Meaning
4. _____	_____	_____	_____
5. _____	_____	_____	_____
6. _____	_____	_____	_____
7. _____	_____	_____	_____
8. _____	_____	_____	_____
9. _____	_____	_____	_____

WRITE ON!

On a separate sheet of paper, write a paragraph on a topic of your choice. Use all six entry words in the paragraph.

Mechanics and Usage

Name _____   Date _____

Dictionary Skills

Dictionary skills are needed in order to use a dictionary efficiently. For each word, a dictionary provides:

- The meanings (definitions) for the word
- The part (or parts) of speech
- A pronunciation
- Example sentences or phrases using the word

Many words have more than one meaning.

  Example: *bed* can be something that you sleep in or it can be where plants are grown

Write two meanings for each word.

  Example: **coat**
    Meaning 1: <u>something worn over the body to keep warm</u>
    Meaning 2: <u>an animal's furry covering</u>

1. **bat**
  Meaning 1: _____
  Meaning 2: _____

2. **saw**
  Meaning 1: _____
  Meaning 2: _____

3. **eye**
  Meaning 1: _____
  Meaning 2: _____

4. **tape**
  Meaning 1: _____
  Meaning 2: _____

5. **record**
  Meaning 1: _____
  Meaning 2: _____

Think back to a time when you were confused about the meaning of a new word. On a separate sheet of paper, write a paragraph about this event.

Name _____   Date _____

Dictionary Skills

Dictionary skills are needed in order to use a dictionary efficiently. For each word, a dictionary provides the following:

- The meanings (definitions) for the word
- The part (or parts) of speech
- A pronunciation
- Example sentences or phrases using the word

Many words have more than one meaning.

    Example: *Cry* can mean something a baby does or a kind of cheer

Write two meanings for each word.

    Example: **button**

            Meaning 1: <u>something that is round with holes in it</u>

            Meaning 2: <u>to fasten one's article of clothing</u>

1. **note**

    Meaning 1: _____

    Meaning 2: _____

2. **cut**

    Meaning 1: _____

    Meaning 2: _____

3. **grade**

    Meaning 1: _____

    Meaning 2: _____

4. **pen**

    Meaning 1: _____

    Meaning 2: _____

5. **rock**

    Meaning 1: _____

    Meaning 2: _____

On a separate sheet of paper, write about a time you earned a good grade or cut yourself badly. Underline any words that have more than one meaning. At the bottom of the page, write the two meanings for each underlined word.

Name _____   Date _____

Dictionary Skills

Dictionary skills are needed in order to use a dictionary efficiently. For each word, a dictionary provides the following:

- The meanings (definitions) for the word
- The part (or parts) of speech
- A pronunciation
- Example sentences or phrases using the word

A dictionary can also be used to find the correct spelling of a word.

   Example: How do I spell *barbieq* correctly?

         I looked in the dictionary and found it on page 295. It is spelled *barbecue*!

Find the correct spelling for each word.

1. *simular* (meaning: the same in appearance) _____

2. *familir* (meaning: reminds one of something)_____

3. *knose* (meaning: to have information about) _____

4. *vaccuumm* (meaning: a cleaning tool)_____

5. *raccoonn* (meaning: a forest animal)_____

6. *ekwipment* (meaning: items used to play sports) _____

7. *sandwitch* (meaning: something to eat)_____

8. *grama* (meaning: your mother or father's mom) _____

9. *cuzin* (meaning: a relative) _____

10. *sutcase* (meaning: used to pack clothing in) _____

11. *calinder* (meaning: used to keep track of the months)_____

12. *bruther* (meaning: a male sibling) _____

On a separate sheet of paper, write a paragraph on the topic of your choice. Rewrite the paragraph misspelling several words. Exchange papers with a classmate. Have the classmate find and underline the misspelled words.

Name _____ Date _____

Dictionary Skills

Dictionary skills are needed in order to use a dictionary efficiently. For each word, a dictionary provides the following:

- The meanings (definitions) for the word
- The part (or parts) of speech
- A pronunciation
- Example sentences or phrases using the word

A dictionary can also be used to find the correct spelling of a word.

Example: How do I spell *airplayne* correctly?

I looked in the dictionary and found it on page 372. It is spelled *airplane!*

Find the correct spelling for each word.

1. *fotograf* (meaning: a printed picture) _____

2. *magzine* (meaning: a printed booklet) _____

3. *trofy* (meaning: a prize) _____

4. *supprise* (meaning: an unexpected event)_____

5. *cort* (meaning: a playing field) _____

6. *techer* (meaning: an instructor) _____

7. *prinsipl* (meaning: the head of the school) _____

8. *arme* (meaning: a military organization) _____

9. *cukie* (meaning: a sweet treat)_____

10. *shugar* (meaning: a sweet ingredient) _____

11. *californya* (meaning: the name of a state) _____

12. *motocycle* (meaning: a two-wheeled bike) _____

What do you do if you don't know how to spell a word? Do you try sounding it out? Guessing how it's spelled? Asking a friend? Or do you look it up? On a separate sheet of paper, write a paragraph telling how you solve spelling mysteries.

Name _____   Date _____

Dictionary Skills

Dictionary skills are needed in order to use a dictionary efficiently. For each word, a dictionary provides the following:

- The meanings (definitions) for the word
- The part (or parts) of speech
- A pronunciation
- Example sentences or phrases using the word

A dictionary can also be used to find the part (or parts) of speech for a particular word. *Squirrel* is a noun if it is naming the furry forest animal.

  Example: The *squirrel* climbed the tree.

Squirrel can also be a verb when talking about saving money or being silly.

  Examples: Grandpa has been *squirreling* away pennies for fifty years!
  Tamra is very *squirrelly*!

PRACTICE

Find the part (or parts) of speech for each word. Use a dictionary.

1. mortgage _____

2. milk _____

3. farm _____

4. travel _____

5. home _____

6. money _____

7. singer _____

8. clothing _____

9. car _____

10. lights _____

WRITE ON!

On a separate sheet of paper, use the words from above with two (or more) parts of speech in a paragraph. Make sure the word is used in all of its forms!

Name _____   Date _____

Dictionary Skills

Dictionary skills are needed in order to use a dictionary efficiently. For each word, a dictionary provides the following:

- The meanings (definitions) for the word
- The part (or parts) of speech
- A pronunciation
- Example sentences or phrases using the word

A dictionary can also be used to find the number of syllables in a word.

Example: **fire** (fi-er) is a two syllable word.

Look up each word in the dictionary. Write the syllabication for each word as well as the number of syllables in the word. Use a dictionary if needed.

Example: **apple**   <u>ap-ple</u>   <u>2 syllables</u>

1. bath _____   _____

2. Cornish _____   _____

3. daughter _____   _____

4. epiphany _____   _____

5. friend _____   _____

6. grandmother _____   _____

7. hustle _____   _____

8. iguana _____   _____

9. juniper _____   _____

10. key _____   _____

11. listener _____   _____

12. motionless _____   _____

Do you know the meanings for all of the words? On a separate sheet of paper, list three words with meanings that you don't know. Look up the words in the dictionary. Write the definitions. Then write a sentence for each word.

ANSWER KEY

Warm-Up 1 (page 7)

1. <u>brother</u>, person
2. <u>friends</u>, person
3. <u>plane</u>, thing
4. <u>cabbages</u>, thing
5. <u>teeth</u>, thing
6. <u>restaurant</u>, place or thing
7. <u>salesman</u>, person
8. <u>photographer</u>, person
9. <u>Tommy</u>, person
10. <u>Milwaukee</u>, place

Check to make sure the students have written appropriate nouns for each category.

Warm-Up 2 (page 8)

1. <u>Eddie</u> was driving the ✧ car to (Chicago.)
2. <u>Mary</u> was working on her medical ✧ degree.
3. Their <u>friends</u> collected ✧ newspapers for recycling.
4. The ✧ alarm was ringing.
5. <u>Dad</u> was in the (kitchen) fixing ✧ dinner.
6. <u>Uncle Teddy</u> was pruning the ✧ trees in the (backyard.)
7. The note ✧ cards were made from construction ✧ paper.
8. The ✧ DVDs were on sale.
9. The ✧ fleas were all over the ✧ animals.
10. The ✧ bed was neatly made.

Check to make sure the students wrote appropriate nouns for each category.

Warm-Up 3 (page 9)

Check to make sure the students wrote an appropriate proper noun. Sample answers:

1. Beck Park
2. Lincoln St.
3. Dr. Cho
4. Mrs. Neeley
5. Easy Paint
6. King
7. New York Diamonds
8. Mrs. Crabtree
9. Value Rite
10. Top Notch
11. Kratt Elementary
12. Mrs. Everson

Warm-Up 4 (page 10)

Check to make sure the students replaced the underlined words with proper nouns. Check to make sure the students rewrote the paragraph correctly.

Warm-Up 5 (page 11)

1. <u>umbrella</u>, singular
2. <u>canopies</u>, plural
3. <u>trophy</u>, singular
4. <u>cups</u>, plural
5. <u>necklace</u>, singular
6. <u>packages</u>, plural
7. <u>Albert Einstein</u>, singular
8. <u>Herbert/Bubba/Walt</u>, plural
9. <u>Morgana</u>, singular
10. <u>troops</u>, plural

Draw a line through the following sentences:

11. She don't know the answer.
13. We was working hard on the project.
15. I is home.
16. Mom and Dad is traveling by train.
18. The girls is baking cookies.

Warm-Up 6 (page 12)

Circle the following sentences: 1, 2, 4, 9, and 10
Check to make sure the students used correct subject-verb agreement for 11–13.

Warm-Up 7 (page 13)

1.–5. Check to make sure the students used correct subject-verb agreement in their sentences.

Warm-Up 8 (page 14)

1. We
2. You
3. He
4. They
5. It
6. I
7. She

My mom decided to make a photo album of our family pictures. <u>She</u> gathered all of her favorite photos. <u>She</u> really likes the one of my dad and me. <u>He</u> was holding a teeny, tiny minnow. <u>I</u> was

holding a humongous fish!
Possessive pronouns (*optional*): My, our, her

Warm-Up 9 (page 15)

1. <u>Larry</u>, He
2. <u>The cat</u>, It
3. <u>The neighbors</u>, They
4. <u>My friends and I</u>, We
5. <u>Patsy</u>, She

The little duckling was climbing the muddy bank of the pond. When <u>the little duckling</u> reached the green grass, <u>the little duckling</u> began waddling. <u>The little duckling</u> waddled to the boy named Henry. <u>Henry</u> picked up the little duckling and carefully carried <u>the little duckling</u> home.

Warm-Up 10 (page 16)

Sample Sentences

1. They went horseback riding.
2. She ran ten laps around the track.
3. It was flatter than a pancake.
4. We are brothers.
5. He drove the RV to the lake.
6. Mary went skydiving last month.
7. Sabrina has the best penmanship!
8. Chelsea and I packed oranges for the customers.
9. Dorothy earned many merit badges.
10. *The Ghost in the Closet* was the best movie!

Warm-Up 11 (page 17)

1. your
2. Her
3. its
4. Our
5. Their, our
6. His
7. My
8. mine
9. theirs
10. hers

The paramedic responded to the call. He helped the woman get into <u>her</u> chair. Then the paramedic wrapped a cuff around <u>her</u> arm to take <u>her</u> blood pressure. He looked at <u>his</u> watch to keep track of the time. <u>Her</u> blood pressure was fine. The paramedic said, "<u>Your</u> blood pressure is good. It is lower than <u>mine</u>!"

Warm-Up 12 (page 18)

1. <u>Mr. and Mrs. Hughes'</u>, Their
2. <u>Sally's</u>, her
3. <u>The tree's</u>, its
4. <u>Mabel's</u>, hers

Mrs. Macy took <u>her</u> children to the local department store. The family stopped at the boys' department. Zach found a pair of pants in <u>his</u> size. Mom said, "The pants are <u>yours</u>!"

"Yeah! The pants are <u>mine</u>!" cheered Zach.

In the girls' department, Barb found a dress in <u>her</u> size. <u>Her</u> little sister grabbed the dress and said, "I want that dress! That dress is <u>mine</u>!"

Mrs. Macy said, "Go get one in <u>your</u> size."

Barb's little sister came back and said, "Here it is. This dress is <u>my</u> size."

Warm-Up 13 (page 19)

Check to make sure the students have used each possessive pronoun correctly in the sentences for 1.–10.

Warm-Up 14 (page 20)

<u>Spot</u> is a <u>dog</u>. <u>Spot</u> lives in a <u>house</u>. <u>Spot</u> has a <u>bowl</u> and a <u>bed</u>. <u>Spot</u> has <u>toys</u>. His favorite is the <u>bone</u>.

Check the paragraph to make sure the students inserted descriptive words before all underlined nouns and then rewrote the paragraph neatly.

Warm-Up 15 (page 21)

1. <u>Pat's</u>, Whose?
2. <u>Seven</u>, How many?
3. <u>Ralph's</u>, Whose?
4. <u>tall</u>, What kind?
5. <u>pretty</u>, What kind?
6. <u>cold</u>, What kind?
7. <u>morning</u>, What kind?
8. <u>Ten</u>, How many?
9. <u>That</u>, Which?
10. <u>This</u>, Which?

ANSWER KEY

Young Ashley went to the circus. She couldn't wait to see all of the exotic animals. Her favorite animals were the gray elephants. Their sparkly costumes shone under the hot lights. Using their flexible trunks, the elephants twirled the fiery batons.

Warm-Up 16 (page 22)
Check to make sure the students have correctly written the sentences.

Warm-Up 17 (page 23)
1. squeakier—sofa and chair
2. shorter—skirt and dress
3. rougher—beard and sandpaper
4. greasier—french fries and baked fries
5. quieter—mouse and rat
6. healthier—Nico and brother
7. tighter—Dad's pants and Uncle Adam's pants
8. brighter—fire and streetlights
9. sharper—knives and pencils
10. harder—Kevin and Wayne
Check to make sure the students wrote the two comparing sentences correctly.

Warm-Up 18 (page 24)
Check to make sure the students wrote the sentences correctly and used the correct form of each adjective.

Warm-Up 19 (page 25)
1. This gym is better than Silver's Gym.
2. This food tastes bad!
3. I have less money in my pocket than in my piggy bank.
4. I have more cookies than Sara,
5. He drove further for the reunion than for the wedding.
6. Who has more puppies than Diego?
The following words should be underlined in the paragraph: *more, fewer, better.*

Warm-Up 20 (page 26)
Check to make sure the students have written their sentences correctly.

Warm-Up 21 (page 27)
1. scariest, three or more
2. neatest, three or more
3. hungrier, two
4. shinier, two
5. sweetest, three or more
6. biggest, three or more
7. messier, two
8. stinkiest, three or more
9. lightest, three or more
10. heavier, two
11.–12. Check to make sure the students have used a correct comparative or superlative adjective for each sentence.

Warm-Up 22 (page 28)
1.–10. Check to make sure the students have used the comparative or superlative adjective correctly in each sentence.
Antoinette took the harder test of her life! She answered fewest than one hundred questions. She made the tinier of marks next to answers she wasn't sure of. She made a littlest smile next to answers she was sure were correct.

Warm-Up 23 (page 29)
1. furthest   2. worst   3. least   4. best
5.–9. Check to make sure the students have used the superlative adjective correctly in each sentence.

Warm-Up 24 (page 30)
Check to make sure the students have compared the items using irregular superlative adjectives.

Warm-Up 25 (page 31)
1. happily   4. rapidly   7. hungrily   9. gently
2. daily   5. quietly   8. beautifully 10. brightly
3. loudly   6. safely
Yvonne dressed nicely for the first day of school. She slowly buttoned her neatly pressed shirt and adjusted her skirt. Her socks were neatly folded over. Yvonne's shoes were carefully shined. Yvonne was finally ready for school.

Warm-Up 26 (page 32)
1. noisily, how
2. daily, when or to what extent
3. finally, when
4. weekly, when or to what extent
5. here, where
6. easily, how
7. monthly, when or to what extent
8. here, where
9. dangerously, how
10. rhythmically, how
Check sentences to make sure students answered appropriately.

Warm-Up 27 (page 33)
1.–10. Check to make sure the students added an appropriate adverb to each sentence.
11.–14. Check to make sure the students wrote three adverbs for each category.

Warm-Up 28 (page 34)
1.–8. Check to make sure the students wrote appropriate sentences.
Jason careful (*carefully*) poured the soda into the cleanly (*clean*) glass. He put a straw into the glass and began noisy (*noisily*) slurping the soda. When he was done, Jason banged the glass onto the table. He burped loud (*loudly*) and left the kitchen.

Warm-Up 29 (page 35)
how: quite, still, almost, just
when: now, soon, yet, then, when
where: around, down, here, there
to what extent: often, twice, very, too

Warm-Up 30 (page 36)
1.–6. Check to make sure the students wrote appropriate sentences. The following adverbs should be underlined in the paragraph: *finally, last night, terrifyingly.*

Warm-Up 31 (page 37)
1.–5. The word *for* in each sentence should be underlined.
The lion was roaring, for it had not eaten for many hours. The zookeeper forgot to feed him, for he was busy taking care of the sick elephant. That night, the zookeeper remembered he had not fed the lion. He raced back to the zoo. The lion was pacing in the cage, for he was very hungry. The zookeeper gave the lion an extra big helping of burgers.

Warm-Up 32 (page 38)
1. The cars and motorcycles drove down the street.
2. The music was loud and had a good beat.
3. The house was old and ugly.
4. Michael dropped the plates and the bowls.
5. The boys screamed when they saw the rat and the mouse.
Ella spent the afternoon practicing the piano. She warmed up on the major scales. She warmed up on the minor scales. / She played her favorite songs. She worked on her fingering on the difficult songs. Then she was done practicing.

Warm-Up 33 (page 39)
Sample sentences:
1. I took neither a sleeping bag nor an air mattress when I went camping.
2. The hospital allows neither cell phones nor walkie-talkies.

3. Neither use sticks nor bricks when building a tree house.
4. The family traveled neither by hot air balloon nor by hang glider.
5. My dad likes neither the desert nor cactus.

Charlene does not like anything. She likes neither hamburgers nor hot dogs. Charlene does not like mustard. When it is time for dessert, Charlene orders neither ice cream nor pudding. Charlene is quite the picky eater!

Warm-Up 34 (page 40)
1. He was asked to whisper in the library, but he was screaming like a maniac.
2. The car was full of gas, but it would not go.
3. The telephone was plugged in, but it never rang.
4. The movie was given good reviews, but nobody was in line to see it.
5. Sally went to the grocery store, but she could not remember what was on the list.

Two sentences to combine: Sophia was sent to her room. She didn't stay in her room.

Warm-Up 35 (page 41)
Sample sentences:
1. You can either be early and pick a good seat or be late and end up standing.
2. Do you want to stand in back or in front?
3. The rocket will go up and reach the stars or crash down into the ground.
4. You can have either chocolate pie or chocolate cake for dessert.
5. I can't remember if Bob likes anchovies or pepperoni on his pizza.

Underline: He wants to be a dentist or a chiropractor.
Circle: Tim knows that he has to study hard or he won't get into a good medical school.

Warm-Up 36 (page 42)
Sample sentences:
1. He had a lot of money, yet he still had to borrow money from his mom.
2. The police car had its red lights flashing, yet nobody would pull over.
3. The donkey had on a hat, yet he still looked angry.
4. Nathan was swinging on the bars, yet it was against the school rules.
5. The rock star held the microphone, yet nobody could hear the words he was singing.
6. The kids were running around the track, yet the coach was not watching.
7. The pet hotel was full of furry customers, yet nobody seemed to mind.
8. Ward and Marianne were on the intercom, yet people were still talking to them.
9. Senator Grace attended the function, yet he was supposed to be at the airport.
10. The tennis shoes were on sale, yet nobody would buy them.

Warm-Up 37 (page 43)
1. Mariska bought an old house, so it needs a lot of work.
2. The real estate agent sold the most houses, so she was given a large bonus.
3. Wilma dropped the cookie crumbs on the ground, so many ants came to get the crumbs.
4. Jason was cold, so he made a fire in the fireplace.
5. Grandpa did not have his hearing aides turned on, so he did not hear the doorbell ringing.

Sentences to be joined in paragraph: The water park was many miles from home. We stopped along the way to get lunch. / Uncle Ben forgot to fill up the gas tank. We ran out of gas.

Warm-Up 38 (page 44)
1. Have you ever been to an amusement park?
2. It was the best birthday ever!
3. After dinner, we went to the park.
4. How many channels does the television get?
5. I had a horrible nightmare!

Warm-Up 39 (page 45)
1. exclamatory—!   3. command—.   5. exclamatory—!
2. interrogatory—?   4. interrogatory—?

Mom made a pitcher of lemonade. (*declarative*) She put the pitcher on the table. (*declarative*) All of a sudden, the cat jumped on the table. (*declarative*) The cat knocked the pitcher of lemonade over! (*exclamatory*) Lemonade went everywhere! (*exclamatory*) What a mess! (*exclamatory*) Mom asked, "Who let the cat in?" (*interrogatory*) My brother and I pointed at each other. (*declarative*)

Warm-Up 40 (page 46)
1. Jason   3. Mrs. Cho   5. Chris
2. Mabel   4. Cameron

Every summer, Jack goes to camp for three weeks. While at camp, Jack goes swimming and canoeing on the lake. He also does different craft activities. This summer, he made plant hangers and wove potholders. Jack loves going to Camp Fun-in-the-Sun!

Warm-Up 41 (page 47)
1. Ellen rode her dirt bike over the sand dune.
2. Alex lit the sparkler on the Fourth of July.
3. Evan works as a police officer.
4. Sean is his brother.
5. Rachel runs a day care center.

Cat and John went to the movies. They took their little girl with them. Their daughter's name is Caitlin. The family went to see the latest picture showing at the local theater. Everyone greatly enjoyed the film.

Warm-Up 42 (page 48)
1.–5. Check to make sure the students correctly completed each sentence.
Three lines under the following: (1)ast, (a)t
Circle with a period after the following words: *beach, starfish*

Warm-Up 43 (page 49)
1.–5. Check to make sure the students correctly completed each interrogatory sentence.
Underline the following sentences: Can you believe that? / Do you even know what spelunking is? / Would you like to be a spelunker?

Warm-Up 44 (page 50)
1. They won the game!
2. I crashed my bike into the big tree!
3. I need help!
4. I see a monster in the backyard!
5. The water is so cold!
Underline the following exclamatory sentences and change the periods to exclamation points. (Answers may vary.)
The fourth batter hit a grand slam!
Our team won the World Series for the first time in fifty years!

Warm-Up 45 (page 51)
1. Wash the car.   4. Stop bouncing the ball.
2. Rake the leaves.   5. Bake the cookies.
3. Be quiet.

ANSWER KEY

Underline the following command sentences: Take the pancake mix, milk, eggs, and oil and stir them in a bowl. / Pour small circles of batter onto a hot griddle and cook until golden brown.

Warm-Up 46 (page 52)
1. interrogatory   3. exclamatory   5. imperative
2. imperative   4. declarative
6.–9. Check to make sure the students have written each type of sentence correctly.

Warm-Up 47 (page 53)
1. Bobby and Joey   4. The quiet boy's name
2. Edie   5. Seventeen people
3. I

Subject in each sentence: *Boyd and Jessica, both kids, Boyd and Jessica, The kids*

Warm-Up 48 (page 54)
1. The green, leafy tree   6. The burly firefighter
2. the logs   7. The patient, painless dentist
3. The washer and dryer   8. Ben
4. Dad   9. Jada and Seline
5. Karen   10. The living room

Warm-Up 49 (page 55)
1. Jerry, Jerry
2. The rotten egg smell; smell
3. The filthy garage; garage
4. The derelict, old factory; factory
5. The beautiful arched window; window
6. The ugly, dead, brown lawn; lawn
7. The old pipes; pipes
8. The experienced pros; pros
9. The old man; man
10. The ringing sound; sound

Warm-Up 50 (page 56)
1. complete subject   6. complete subject
2. simple subject   7. simple subject
3. simple subject   8. simple subject
4. complete subject   9. simple subject
5. complete subject   10. complete subject

Warm-Up 51 (page 57)
1. Scotty has many friends.
2. Jill and Riley played air hockey.
3. The book was exciting to read.
4. The warm, fuzzy jacket was hanging on the hook.
5. Cassandra jumped over the hoop.
   Hercules is a boxer puppy. He has long, skinny legs. Hercules loves to run around the house. He jumps on people. Hercules is a very active puppy!

Warm-Up 52 (page 58)
1.–10. Check to make sure the students have the complete predicate for each sentence.

Warm-Up 53 (page 59)
1. Dorothy is the manager for many rock stars.
2. The grapevines are full of ripe grapes.
3. The senator and her husband listened to the bagpipes.
4. The party was held at the local ice rink.
5. Let's talk about the new job.
6. Tell us about growing lettuce.
7. The desert is full of different kinds of life.
8. Many people attended the performance.

9. The bridge spanned the great river.
10. The computer was making funny noises.

Warm-Up 54 (page 60)
1. simple predicate   6. simple predicate
2. simple predicate   7. simple predicate
3. complete/simple predicate 8. simple predicate
4. complete predicate   9. complete/simple predicate
5. complete predicate   10. complete predicate

Warm-Up 55 (page 61)
Sentences 2, 3, and 5 should be circled.
   Danny met his friend at the local nursery. Danny and his friend bought many brightly-colored flowers and several bags of potting soil and a couple of different ceramic pots for the backyard. At the register, Danny paid for the items and Danny and his friend loaded the items into the back of the pick-up truck and drove home.

Warm-Up 56 (page 62)
1. Bob and Jay are brothers. Both of them are firefighters. They each drive red trucks.
2. The blankets are in the cedar chest. The linens are in the cupboard. The pillows are on the shelf in the closet.
3. Jim is a veterinarian. He takes care of all kinds of animals. He also boards animals overnight.
4. The carpenter cut the board in half. He placed the board against the wall. He hammered three nails into the board.

Warm-Up 57 (page 63)
Numbers 1, 4, 5, 8, and 9 should be circled.
   Nicole likes to design clothing. She picked out. She decided to make a dress. The pattern. She carefully cut around the pins. Then Nicole removed the pins and sewed the seams. Was done!

Warm-Up 58 (page 64)
1. complete sentence   6. complete sentence
2 sentence fragment   7. complete sentence
3 sentence fragment   8. sentence fragment
4. sentence fragment   9. sentence fragment
5. sentence fragment   10. sentence fragment
   The following sentences should be underlined: He has appeared. Broke many bones. Horse kicked.

Warm-Up 59 (page 65)
Sample sentences:
1. I am never on time for   5. Nobody worked hard in
   school.   the yard.
2. Nobody passed the test.   6. No dogs were at the dog
3. I cannot hear you.   park.
4. I have no marbles.
   Negative sentences in paragraph: Not only did he sleep through his alarm, he also had hardly enough time to eat breakfast. Then his car wouldn't start and he barely made it to work. Dennis hoped he would never have another day like this again.

Warm-Up 60 (page 66)
1. My wife does not want a new roof.
2. The house is not done.
3. She did not build the tree house.
4. I can barely fit into my jeans.
5. Nobody gave me a present.
6. I have never been on a cruise.
7. Hardly anybody is listening.
8. The scratch was barely noticeable.
9. Only a few rides are for children.
10. I have nothing.
   Ming is a great speed skater. Ming hardly ever falls. He never skates into the walls. Nobody else skates as well as Ming!

Warm-Up 61 (page 67)
1. I <u>don't</u> want <u>nothing</u>. / I want something.
2. <u>Only</u> a few gave <u>nothing</u>. / Some people gave something.
3. <u>Barely</u> <u>no one</u> got away. / Almost everyone got away.
4. There was <u>hardly</u> <u>nothing</u> left to eat. / There was something left to eat.
5. <u>Barely</u> <u>nobody</u> came to the party. / A few people came to the party.

Warm-Up 62 (page 68)
1. I don't have any money. OR I have no money.
2. She is not speaking to me.
3. That answer is never correct.
4. I can barely cut through the fabric.
5. John does not (or doesn't) know anybody.
6. Caitlin never has any.
7. Nobody heard the meowing cat.
8. She can hardly wait!
9. Mark said that he doesn't need any help.
10. Dad can barely get any sleep.

Warm-Up 63 (page 69)
1. A   3. A   5. C   7. A   9. A
2. B   4. A   6. C   8. A   10. A

Warm-Up 64 (page 70)
1. B   3. B   5. C   7. B   9. B   11. to   13. too   15. too
2. A   4. C   6. B   8. C   10. B   12. to   14. to

Warm-Up 65 (page 71)
1. adjective   4. adjective   7. noun   9. adjective
2. adjective   5. adjective   8. adjective   10. noun
3. adjective   6. adjective
11.–12. Check to make sure the students have written the
        sentences correctly.

Warm-Up 66 (page 72)
1. to   3. two   5. too   7. too   9. to
2. too   4. two   6. to   8. two   10. too

I have ~~to~~ (*two*) dogs. Their names are Gracie and Bea. Gracie has a beautiful red coat. Bea is beautiful, ~~two~~ (*too*). She is fawn and white. The ~~too~~ (*two*) dogs are littermate sisters. This means the ~~too~~ (*two*) of them are from the same litter. (A litter is the puppies that a mother dog has. A mother dog might have one or ~~to~~ (*two*) litters each year.) The dogs are ~~two~~ (*too*) funny to watch, but they also give me many headaches, ~~to~~ (*too*).

Warm-Up 67 (page 73)
1. too   3. two   5. to   7. two
2. too   4. to   6. too, to 8. to
9.–11. Check to make sure the students have written the
       sentences correctly.

Warm-Up 68 (page 74)
1. <u>There</u>, location   6. <u>there</u>, location
2. <u>there</u>, location   7. <u>there</u>, location
3. <u>Their</u>, ownership   8. <u>Their</u>, ownership
4. <u>their</u>, ownership   9. <u>their</u>, ownership
5. <u>Their</u>, ownership   10. <u>Their</u>, ownership

Steve and I went to camp. While we were <u>there</u>, we learned to do many new things. The camp leader taught us how to canoe, build a fire, and make a shelter. While <u>there</u>, we also met three brothers. <u>Their</u> names were Billy, Bobby, and Benny. This was <u>their</u> first time at camp, too. Steve and I were glad that we went <u>there</u> this summer.

Warm-Up 69 (page 75)
1. Their   3. their   5. their   7. they're   9. their
2. They're 4. there   6. their   8. Their   10. their
11.–13. Check to make sure the students have written the sentences.

Warm-Up 70 (page 76)
1. They're   4. their   7. their   10. their
2. their   5. there   8. They're, there
3. There   6. there   9. their

<u>Their</u> boat is painted bright blue. Bright blue is <u>their</u> favorite color. The boat is over <u>there</u> by the canoe. <u>They're</u> lucky to have <u>their</u> own boat. <u>They're</u> going to take <u>their</u> boat out today. If we get over <u>there</u>, we can go, too!

Warm-Up 71 (page 77)
1. Our   3. our   5. are   7. are   9. are
2. are   4. our   6. our   8. are   10. our

<u>Our</u> classes decided to make a float for <u>our</u> town's parade. We <u>are</u> going to use different-colored flowers, streamers, and tissue paper. <u>Our</u> families will help us put the decorations on <u>our</u> float. When we <u>are</u> done, <u>our</u> float will be the best looking one in the parade!

Warm-Up 72 (page 78)
1. hour   3. Are   5. Our   7. our
2. our   4. are   6. hour   8. are

Next month, ~~are~~ (*our*) class will go on a field trip. We ~~hour~~ (*are*) going to the local museum. We will arrive the very ~~our~~ (*hour*) the museum opens. The museum is the first one to exhibit *Cowboys of the Wild West*. This is a very famous exhibit, and ~~hour~~ (*our*) class is excited to view it. Many of ~~are~~ (*our*) parents will be going with us. They said that they wanted to be ~~hour~~ (*our*) chaperones, but we know the parents ~~our~~ (*are*) also excited to see the cowboy exhibit.

Warm-Up 73 (page 79)
1. know   4. no   7. know   10. No   13. know
2. know   5. no   8. no   11. know   14. knows
3. no   6. know   9. know   12. no   15. no

Warm-Up 74 (page 80)
1. your   3. You're   5. your   7. your
2. You're   4. Your   6. Your   8. your

I pick you and Drew to be on my team. ~~Your~~ (*You're*) both the best players in the class. With ~~you're~~ (*your*) help, I know we can win the play-offs at lunchtime. Here is the plan. You will kick the ball hard and then get on base. Then Drew will kick next and she will kick the ball hard, too. Once ~~your~~ (*you're*) both on base, I know you will be able to make it home and score the winning runs!

Warm-Up 75 (page 81)
1. its   4. its   7. It's   10. its   13. its   16. It's
2. It's   5. It's   8. it's   11. its   14. Its
3. It's   6. its   9. its   12. its   15. its

Warm-Up 76 (page 82)
1. believed   4. danced   7. filling
2. brushing   5. worked   8. painted
3. staying   6. changed
Check to make sure the students changed the verbs so that they are all in the same tense. (Answers could be present tense.)

(*Sample of Past Tense*) Mom and Dad <u>planned</u> our family vacation. They <u>thought</u> about going to a ghost town. We <u>would</u> rather go to a dude ranch. Mom and Dad <u>were</u> sure that we <u>will like</u> (*would*) the ghost town. Mom <u>is calling</u> (*called*) and <u>is making</u> (*made*) the reservations.

Warm-Up 77 (page 83)
Marvin ~~hosting~~ (*hosts* OR *is hosting*) his own talk show on the public access channel. During each broadcast, Marvin interviews local dignitaries, shows film clips, and chats with kids from the local schools. Marvin ~~uses~~ (*used*) to have a segment where kids ~~showing~~ (*showed*) the latest skateboard moves. It wasn't a

good idea because the skateboarders had a hard time ~~controlled~~ (*controlling*) the skateboards. Many pieces of camera equipment and stage items were broken. Marvin is now ~~thinked~~ (*thinking*) of ~~haved~~ (*having*) a segment called "Things to Cook While Playing Soccer." What do you think of this idea?

1.–3. Check to make sure the students wrote the words and definitions for three words.

Warm-Up 78 (page 84)

1. practices   3. prepares   5. turns   7. speaks   9. surf
2. waxes   4. talk   6. frost   8. look   10. knits

Warm-Up 79 (page 85)

1. Jeff and Donna have an early morning paper route.
2. Together, they fold the papers and put them into their delivery bags.
3. Jeff delivers the newspapers to the homes on the left side of the street.
4. The two kids are done with their route in no time!

Warm-Up 80 (page 86)

1. jumps, present   5. takes, present   9. chased, past
2. kicked, past   6. liked, past   10. helps, present
3. eats, present   7. catches, present
4. climbs, present   8. stopped, past

Warm-Up 81 (page 87)

Katy climbs mountains on the weekend. On Friday night, Katy checks her climbing equipment to make sure that she has everything she needs: helmet, shoes, ropes, backpack, water, snacks, first-aid kit, and a change of clothes. In the morning, Katy rides her bike to the nearby mountain and begins climbing. One day, she hopes to scale the tallest mountains in the world. (Present)

Katy climbed mountains on the weekend. On Friday night, Katy checked her climbing equipment to make sure that she had everything she needed: helmet, shoes, ropes, backpack, water, snacks, first-aid kit, and a change of clothes. In the morning, Katy rode her bike to the nearby mountain and began climbing. One day, she hoped to scale the tallest mountains in the world. (Past)

Warm-Up 82 (page 88)

1. re/do, 2, to do again
2. re/read, 2, to read again
3. re/fill, 2, to fill again
4. re/made, 2, made again
5. re/play, 2, to play again
6. play/ful, 2, full of play
7. cheer/ful, 2, full of cheer
8. eye/ful, 2, filling the eye
9. taste/ful, 2, full of taste
10. fright/ful, 2, full of fright

Warm-Up 83 (page 89)

1. un/hap/py, 3, not happy
2. pre/test, 2, a test before the actual test
3. pre/view, 2, to see something before it is actually played or seen
4. meat/less, 2, without meat
5. age/less, 2, without age
6. play/er, 2, person who plays
7. driv/er, 2, person who drives
8. weight/less, 2, without weight

Warm-Up 84 (page 90)

1. o/ver/bid, 3, pay too much
2. lone/li/ness, 3, a state of being lonely
3. mid/course, 2, in the middle of something
4. imp/ish, 2, like an imp
5. re/play, 2, to play again
6. child/ish, 2, childlike or like a child
7. mid/day, 2, middle of the day

8. sad/ness, 2, state of being sad
9. mid/life, 2, middle of one's life

Warm-Up 85 (page 91)

1. un/know/ing   4. hope/ful/ly   7. cheer/ful/ly
2. dis/taste/ful   5. un/friend/ly   8. re/check/ing
3. un/like/ly   6. un/end/ing

Underline the following words in the paragraph: *grocery, magazines,* and *customers.*

Warm-Up 86 (page 92)

2. re/pay/ment   7. re/fin/ish/ing
3. un/for/get/ta/ble   8. un/be/liev/able
6. sad/ness   12. re/group/ing

Warm-Up 87 (page 93)

1. stap/ler   6. hol/low   11. mir/ror   16. mon/key
2. blan/ket   7. can/dy   12. pup/py   17. rab/bit
3. pil/low   8. pen/cil   13. kit/ten   18. but/ton
4. win/dow   9. mar/ker   14. pas/ture   19. tor/so
5. cur/tain   10. slip/per   15. car/pet   20. mit/ten

Check to make sure the students have written three more words that fit the pattern.

Warm-Up 88 (page 94)

Margene is taking an auto repair class. She studies all kinds of things about cars. In the first class, the students learned the names for the different parts outside of the car: tires, hubcaps, trunk, hood, roof, door, window, and gas cap. This week, the students will study about what is under the hood. Margene was amazed at all of the parts that are needed to make a car actually drive.

1. Mar/gene   3. out/side   5. un/der   7. ac/tu/al/ly
2. dif/fer/ent   4. hub/caps   6. win/dow

Warm-Up 89 (page 95)

1. tu/na   5. col/or   9. lil/y   13. pi/rate
2. mo/tel   6. sol/id   10. sat/in   14. u/nique
3. re/mote   7. e/rase   11. li/lac   15. sha/dy
4. pa/per   8. i/ris   12. med/ic   16. po/ny

The following words in paragraph should be underlined: *favorite, overhauled.*

Warm-Up 90 (page 96)

Our family has a dog named Rufus. Rufus is a pedigree. Over the weekend, Rufus entered a national dog show. He was so excited to be in the center ring and have everyone's eyes on him. Rufus showed his stuff. He strutted around the ring, struck his poses, and followed all of his commands. Rufus didn't win first place, but he did win the runner-up position.

1. Ru/fus   3. a/round
2. O/ver   4. po/si/tion

Warm-Up 91 (page 97)

1. col/or   5. po/ny   9. im/age   13. ol/ive
2. grav/el   6. gar/ish   10. cav/ern   14. va/cant
3. lil/y   7. shov/el   11. clos/et   15. fam/ish
4. sha/dy   8. lim/it   12. frol/ic   16. ho/tel

Heidi has a new dog. The dog's name was Lovie, but Heidi changed it to Lily. She thought Lily was a better fit. Lily is a white color. She loves to have her soft fur brushed and her ears cleaned. Her chew toy is made of linen. She hides it in the closet. Lily is the best dog!

Warm-Up 92 (page 98)

Billy was so excited. Today was his seventh birthday. For breakfast, his mom made pancakes with syrup. Billy's pancakes spelled out his name. For lunch, his dad took him to the local pizza place. Billy ordered pepperoni pizza with <u>chili</u> peppers. For dinner, his grandparents came over. Grandpa barbecued hot dogs. After dinner, Billy got to blow out the candles on his birthday cake. It was <u>devil's</u> food cake with <u>lemon</u> frosting. It was a great day!

1. sev/enth   3. chil/i   5. lem/on
2. syr/up   4. dev/il's

Warm-Up 93 (page 99)

1. i/ci/cle	6. re/cy/cle	11. pick/le	16. i/dle
2. fum/ble	7. cy/cle	12. trick/le	17. ap/ple
3. rub/ble	8. bum/ble	13. pur/ple	18. tur/tle
4. mum/ble	9. rum/ble	14. lit/tle	19. bub/ble
5. stum/ble	10. tum/ble	15. un/cle	20. ea/gle

Warm-Up 94 (page 100)

My favorite hobby is metal detecting. I like to go metal detecting at my favorite place. It's near the <u>castle</u>. It's not really a <u>castle</u> anymore. It's just a bunch of <u>rubble</u>. But it looks like it might have been a <u>castle</u> at one time. Last time I went metal detecting, I found a nickel, a <u>purple</u> <u>turtle</u> made from metal, and a horn from a <u>tricycle</u>. While I haven't found anything worth a lot yet, I still like the thrill of the hunt.

1. cas/tle   3. pur/ple   5. tri/cy/cle
2. rub/ble   4. tur/tle

Warm-Up 95 (page 101)

1. fire/fight/er   4. wa/ter/mel/on   7. down/stairs
2. snow/man   5. Grand/ma   8. eye/balls
3. tur/tle/necks   6. key/board

When I grow up, I want to be a secret agent. I am really good at wearing disguises and going <u>undercover</u>. I always wear an <u>overcoat</u> with many pockets. In the pockets, I keep the many tools I need in order to do my job well. I carry a <u>spyglass</u>, funny <u>eyeglasses</u>, a pair of <u>overalls</u>, and some socks. When spying on <u>somebody</u>, I never ring the <u>doorbell</u>. Instead, I peek into windows or follow them on my <u>motorcycle</u>. I will be a fantastic secret agent!

Warm-Up 96 (page 102)

Our troop took a boat out onto the ocean. The boat was unique, because it had a glass bottom. Through the glass bottom, our troop could see all of the amazing sea creatures. Gary saw a <u>seahorse</u>. It was very unusual looking. The twins said that they saw a <u>hammerhead</u> shark, but the troop leader said that it was a <u>jellyfish</u>. The twins said that they were confused, because they weren't wearing their <u>eyeglasses</u>. Steve saw an octopus with its eggs. The eggs looked like little <u>rainbows</u>. We had a great time at the <u>seaside</u>.

1. sea/horse   3. jel/ly/fish   5. rain/bows
2. ham/mer/head   4. eye/glass/es   6. sea/side

Warm-Up 97 (page 103)

1. heck/le	5. tick/ling	9. fax/ing	13. ox/en
2. lock/et	6. check/ers	10. max/i/mum	14. ax/es
3. tack/le	7. mix/ing	11. tick/ets	15. thick/en
4. nick/el	8. six/es	12. thick/et	

Warm-Up 98 (page 104)

When my dad was in college, he drove a <u>taxi</u> to pay the bills. His <u>taxi</u> took people from all over the world. He drove them to both new and old parts of the city. My dad was <u>tickled</u> to learn how to greet people in over thirty different languages. One fare even gave him a <u>nickel</u> for every greeting that my dad said. My dad was <u>lucky</u>. He never once had an accident or was given a <u>ticket</u> while driving the <u>taxi</u>.

1. tax/i   3. nick/el   5. tick/et
2. tick/led   4. luck/y

Warm-Up 99 (page 105)

1. sl<u>ee</u>ve	5. v<u>oi</u>d	9. gr<u>ee</u>n	13. di/<u>e</u>t
2. lo/t<u>io</u>n	6. c<u>oi</u>n	10. gui/tar	14. fact/<u>u/a</u>l
3. h<u>ea</u>d	7. vi/<u>o</u>/lent	11. fl<u>oo</u>r	15. vid/<u>e</u>/o
4. b<u>e</u>/ing	8. li/<u>o</u>n	12. l<u>ea</u>/ther	16. i/<u>o</u>/ta

Brian just started taking <u>gutar</u> (*guitar*) lessons from his friend Larry. At the beginning of each lesson, Brian watches a <u>vidyo</u> (*video*) that shows the correct finger positions. Brian picks up his guitar and puts the leather strap around his neck. Then Brian strums the strings and makes a lot of <u>noyse</u> (*noise*). After he is done <u>beeing</u> (*being*) a rock star, the <u>actuel</u> (*actual*) lesson begins.

Warm-Up 100 (page 106)

Our school is participating in the fitness challenge. We met at the <u>stadium</u> to get weighed in before the competition began. As part of the competition, we will watch our <u>diet</u>. Most of us will start eating <u>cereal</u> for breakfast. Our parents are <u>actually</u> surprised that we are willing to give up junk food.

1. sta/di/um   2. di/et   3. ce/re/al   4. ac/tu/al/ly

Warm-Up 101 (page 107)

1. el/e/ments	5. cav/i/ar
2. dig/i/tal	6. hy/e/na
3. el/e/phant	7. an/i/mal
4. math/e/mat/i/cal	8. priv/i/lege
9. man/u/script	
10. flex/i/ble	

Check to make sure the students have written three other words that fit the rule.

Warm-Up 102 (page 108)

<u>Olivia</u> is a <u>creative</u> person. She once made a <u>chrysalis</u> out of <u>flexible</u> wire and tissue paper. She then made the <u>animal</u> it would become, a butterfly, using <u>similar</u> materials. <u>Olivia</u> then made their <u>habitat</u> including all of the important <u>elements</u>: plants, nectar, grass, sun, and water. It was a beautiful exhibit.

1. O/liv/i/a   4. flex/i/ble   7. hab/i/tat
2. cre/a/tive   5. an/i/mal   8. el/e/ments
3. chrys/a/lis   6. sim/i/lar

Warm-Up 103 (page 109)

1. re/peat	8. ex/cuse	15. be/neath
2. de/fend	9. re/call	16. ex/pand
3. ex/it	10. ex/po	17. de/sign
4. ex/hale	11. ex/er/cise	18. be/friend
5. re/play	12. de/tail	19. re/build
6. re/cy/cle	13. re/made	20. ex/ceed
7. ex/plore	14. ex/tinct	

Check to make sure the students have written three other words that fit the rule.

Warm-Up 104 (page 110)

Joshua likes to <u>exercise</u> every day. He says he does it <u>because</u> it feels good and helps him to <u>relax</u> after a hard day at school. When he <u>begins</u> his <u>exercises</u>, he warms up with a few stretches. Then he <u>decides</u> if he is going to go jogging, run on the treadmill, or jump on the trampoline. He stops <u>exercising</u> when he feels <u>exhausted</u>. Then he drinks plenty of water so that he doesn't <u>become</u> <u>dehydrated</u>.

1. ex/er/cise   5. ex/er/cis/es   8. ex/haust/ed
2. be/cause   6. de/cides   9. be/come
3. re/lax   7. ex/er/cis/ing   10. de/hy/drat/ed
4. be/gins

Warm-Up 105 (page 111)

1. act/ed	10. tast/ed	15. light/ed
4. squint/ed	11. heat/ed	17. rat/ed
5. part/ed	12. foot/ed	18. load/ed
6. dent/ed	13. crowd/ed	19. faint/ed
7. print/ed	14. squirt/ed	20. dart/ed

Check to make sure the students write three more words that fit the rule.

Warm-Up 106 (page 112)

The following words should be underlined in the paragraph: *attempted, floated, heated*.

1. at/tempt/ed	2. float/ed	3. heat/ed

Warm-Up 107 (page 113)

1. lev/el	6. cru/el	11. ment/al	16. hab/it/u/al
2. mod/el	7. herb/al	12. pet/al	17. flor/al
3. port/al	8. laur/el	13. leg/al	18. jew/el
4. reg/al	9. mu/tu/al	14. tot/al	19. nick/el
5. fer/al	10. ped/al	15. gru/el	20. med/al

Check to make sure the students have written three words that rhyme with *legal* and have written a sentence about their spellings and the rule.

Warm-Up 108 (page 114)

For Halloween, we dressed up in our <u>usual</u> costumes. My sister went as a <u>model</u>. My brother went as a <u>legal</u> wiz. I went as a daisy, complete with a million <u>petals</u>. Once we had our <u>novel</u> costumes on, our dad took us out trick-or-treating. Our first stop was Old Man Greer's house. He always gives out <u>nickels</u> instead of candy. He said that I should be in a <u>floral</u> display and that my brother should win a <u>medal</u> for being a lawyer. By <u>mutual</u> agreement, our next stop was Mrs. <u>Jewel's</u> house. She gives out the best treats! By the end of the evening, our bags were full of candy, and we were tired!

1. u/su/al	4. pet/als	7. flor/al	9. mu/tu/al
2. mod/el	5. nov/el	8. med/al	10. Jew/el's
3. leg/al	6. nick/els		

Warm-Up 109 (page 115)

1. sta/tion	8. ad/di/tion	15. de/par/ture
2. sta/ture	9. at/ten/tion	16. mix/ture
3. cre/a/tion	10. fea/ture	17. sec/tion
4. na/ture	11. ra/tion	18. no/tion
5. temp/er/a/ture	12. ma/ture	19. lec/ture
6. cau/tion	13. pas/ture	20. po/tion
7. di/rec/tion	14. tex/ture	

21.–23. Check to make sure the students have selected three words and have written their definitions.

Warm-Up 110 (page 116)

Kenny works on a <u>demolition</u> crew. Each morning, Kenny reports to his <u>station</u> to get the day's <u>directions</u>. He has to pay careful <u>attention</u> so that he and his crew do not destroy the wrong building. One time, Kenny got the <u>directions</u> wrong and ended up at a <u>pasture</u> full of sheep! He was given a big <u>lecture</u> by the manager.

1. dem/o/li/tion	3. di/rec/tions	5. pas/ture
2. sta/tion	4. at/ten/tion	6. lec/ture

Warm-Up 111 (page 117)

1. question	6. quickly	11. quill
2. quiet	7. quarter	12. racquet
3. quit	8. equipment	13. queasy
4. quiz	9. liquid	14. equal
5. request	10. sequel	15. earthquake

Warm-Up 112 (page 118)

Every <u>qarter</u> (*quarter*), our teacher likes to give us a pop <u>qiz</u> (*quiz*). The quiz has twenty questions on everything that we have covered. The teacher has us place our desks an <u>eqal</u> (*equal*) distance apart. Then she always gives us some kind of inspirational <u>qote</u> (*quote*), the class gets <u>qiet</u> (*quiet*), and the quiz begins. It is <u>qickly</u> (*quickly*) over until the sequel next quarter!

1. quart/er	3. e/qual	5. qui/et
2. quiz	4. quote	6. quick/ly

7.–10. Check to make sure the students have written a definition for each word.

Warm-Up 113 (page 119)

1. saving	6. likable	11. lacing	16. dine
2. hiding	7. taming	12. valuable	17. pave
3. livable	8. reusing	13. leave	18. rough
4. raking	9. curable	14. move	19. mope
5. drivable	10. baking	15. come	20. stripe

Warm-Up 114 (page 120)

Mitchell loves <u>bakeing</u> (*baking*) during his free time. For the school bake sale, Mitchell was in his element. He spent the morning <u>makying</u> (*making*) different kinds of cupcakes. Mitchell spent a lot of time <u>decorateing</u> (*decorating*) the cupcakes <u>useing</u> (*using*) sprinkles, frosting, and chocolate candies. After lunch, Mitchell made cookies. He made sugar cookies, peanut butter cookies, and chocolate chip cookies. All of the cookies were Mitchell's favorites!

1. bak/ing 2. mak/ing 3. dec/o/rat/ing 4. us/ing

5.–8. Check to make sure the students have written a definition for each word.

Warm-Up 115 (page 121)

1. studied	3. trying	5. graying	7. sloppily
2. luckily	4. copying	6. staying	8. buried

We are going to the local canyon. We are <u>tring</u> (*trying*) to get a bus that will hold all of our class, but we are <u>haveing</u> (*having*) a difficult time. Last year, some of the kids <u>staied</u> (*stayed*) behind because there wasn't enough room on the bus. We don't want that to happen again. <u>Luckyily</u> (*Luckily*), one of the classmates' parents owns a large van and can take the extra kids!

Warm-Up 116 (page 122)

I am <u>studing</u> (*studying*) to be a photographer like my Aunt Fran. She began <u>takeing</u> (*taking*) photographs at my age. She made her first camera <u>useing</u> (*using*) an oatmeal box, tin foil, and photography paper. She shared with me her first photos, and they were really <u>amazeing</u> (*amazing*). Later, my aunt went to college and majored in photography. She took pictures for the school paper. After <u>graduateing</u> (*graduating*) from college, my aunt worked for a local newspaper before she opened her own business. I am <u>hopeing</u> (*hoping*) that I will be a great photographer like my aunt!

1. study/ing	3. us/ing	5. grad/u/at/ing
2. tak/ing	4. a/maz/ing	6. hop/ing

7.–10. Check to make sure the students have written a definition for each word.

Warm-Up 117 (page 123)

1. sandwiches	5. taxes	9. stashes
2. dots	6. boxes	10. rashes
3. trucks	7. sacks	11. eyelashes
4. shoulders	8. messes	12. crashes

13.–14. Check to make sure the students have written three other words that fit each rule.

ANSWER KEY

Warm-Up 118 (page 124)

1. ceiling	4. field	7. receipt	10. chief
2. yield	5. believe	8. fierce	11. niece
3. shield	6. receive	9. deceive	12. relieve

We live in a really old house. Every time it rains, our <u>ceeling</u> (*ceiling*) leaks. It's like it is raining right inside the house. We put out every pot and bucket that we have in order to <u>sheeld</u> (*shield*) the carpets from the rain. But it doesn't help. By the time the rain is over, our carpet is like a soggy football <u>feeld</u> (*field*). We will be <u>releeved</u> (*relieved*) when we finally get the roof fixed!

Warm-Up 119 (page 125)

1. neighbor	5. eight	9. reindeer	13. beige
2. veil	6. sleigh	10. reign	14. neigh
3. foreign	7. height	11. leisure	
4. freight	8. weight	12. veins	

Rhyming words: sleigh/neigh, reign/vein, eight/freight/weight

Warm-Up 120 (page 126)

Check to make sure the students wrote each title correctly.

Underline the following titles: <u>The Lion and the Mouse</u>, <u>Jump Off the High Cliff</u>, and <u>I Love Trains</u>

Warm-Up 121 (page 127)

1. I watched the street performance of <u>A Chocolate Raindrop</u>.
2. The song "Music for Hippies" is a number one hit!
3. For seventeen years, <u>Dogs!</u> was a Broadway hit!
4. "At the End of the Day" is a very sad poem.
5. <u>Where is My Dog?</u> is the name of the play.

Capitalize and underline the following: <u>My Uncle Is an Alien</u>, <u>Your Momma Ate a Train</u>, <u>Garlic in My Salad</u>

Warm-Up 122 (page 128)

1. "Where is my surfboard?" asked Mavis.
4. "I have three teenage sons," said Nan.
5. "I have a messy style," agreed Ryan.

Warm-Up 123 (page 129)

1. Walter said, "I have three pets."
2. "My phone is ringing!" exclaimed Marsha.
3. "My bunny's name is Smokey," Heidi said.
4. Mark said, "My last name is Smith."
5. Grandpa asked, "Do you want to go to Maryland?"
6. Mom sighed, "I love red cars."
7. Sissy asked, "Who sat in my beanbag chair?"

Warm-Up 124 (page 130)

1. Paul ran down the street screaming, "I saw a hamster!"
2. Dr. Taylor said, "Eat an apple every day."
3. Mom asked, "Did you write it on the calendar?"
4. Grandma said, "I made the wooden train."
5. Linda asked, "Who made this mess?"
6. Jeff and Brandon both shouted, "Hurray!"

Check to make sure the two sentences each student wrote are correct.

Warm-Up 125 (page 131)

Uncle Joe came to spend the day with us. Uncle Joe asked, "What would you two chaps like to do today?"

I said, "Let's go to the park and play soccer!"

My little brother said, "No! I want to go rollerblading."

Uncle Joe laughed and said, "I know what we will do. We'll play soccer before lunch and go rollerblading after lunch!"

My little brother and I said, "Great idea, Uncle Joe!"

Warm-Up 126 (page 132)

"Where is the dog?" asked Robert. "I can't find her and I've looked everywhere!"

"Have you checked outside?" asked Ruby.

"Yes, I even looked in her doghouse," replied Robert.

"Well, maybe she's out in the garage," suggested Ruby.

"Good thinking, Ruby. I will check there next," said Robert.

Warm-Up 127 (page 133)

Circle the following sentences: 1, 3, 4, 5, 7, 8, 9

Warm-Up 128 (page 134)

Check to make sure the students have written an independent clause for each topic.

Warm-Up 129 (page 135)

1. formal, colon	6. informal, comma
2. informal, comma	7. informal, comma
3. informal, comma	8. formal, colon
4. formal, colon	9. informal, comma
5. formal, colon	10. informal, comma

Warm-Up 130 (page 136)

1.–5. Check to make sure students added the colon between the word and the definition.

6.–10. Check to make sure the students have written a definition for each word and have remembered to add the colon between the word and the definition.

The following sentence has a colon in it—It said, "kennel: a cage for dogs."

Warm-Up 131 (page 137)

1. statement	5. statement	9. statement
2. statement	6. statement	10. command
3. command	7. statement	
4. statement	8. command	

Sample sentences:

11. Do not talk in the library.
12. Stop at the sign.
13. Nancy will go home after the movie.
14. Barney will sweep the sidewalk.

Warm-Up 132 (page 138)

Check to make sure the students have written five statements and five commands.

Command sentences that should be circled:

"Get two sticks and tie them together," said Dad.

"Now," said Dad, "tie a piece of string so that it goes around the outside of the sticks."

The rest of the sentences should be underlined.

Warm-Up 133 (page 139)

1. <u>Do you want to go to the store?</u>
3. <u>Where is Matilda?</u>
6. <u>Have you ever been to the mountains?</u>
7. <u>What is peach fuzz?</u>
9. <u>Do you have a big family?</u>
11.–12. Check to make sure the students have written two questions correctly.

Warm-Up 134 (page 140)

Check to make sure the students have written questions for each topic. The following sentences should be circled: "Are you sure that's a good idea?" / "Is anybody else getting scared?" / "Are you?" / "What do you think?"

Warm-Up 135 (page 141)

The following sentences should be circled:

1. He won with the fastest time ever.
2. Jerome made the most delicious cake.

ANSWER KEY

3 I love that design.
4. That music is so loud.
5. There's Fido.
6. The fire engine was going to the largest fire ever.
7. Be careful.
8. Don't look directly at the sun.
9. Your hair is so long.
10. All of the tires were flat.
11.–15. Check to make sure the students have written exclamatory sentences.

Warm-Up 136 (page 142)
The following sentences should be circled: He was almost hit by the semitruck. / It was smashed to smithereens.
Check to make sure the students have rewritten the paragraph correctly, adding exclamation points after the two sentences above.

Warm-Up 137 (page 143)

1. Mr.	4. Capt.	7. Mrs.	10. Sgt.	13. St.
2. yd.	5. Ln.	8. mi.	11. Sr.	14. St.
3. Jr.	6. Ave.	9. ft.	12. Dr.	15. in.

Last weekend, my family and I went camping at <u>Mount</u> Shasta. We pitched our tents at the campground. The tents were about three <u>feet</u> apart. We then walked about half a <u>mile</u> down the path to Lake Full-of-Water. We caught many fish. We walked back up Mulberry <u>Road</u> and spread the fish out over two <u>yards</u> of clothesline. We built a fire under the clothesline about six <u>inches</u> under the fish. <u>Captain</u> White came by to make sure we were following the local fire rules. We had a great time camping!

Warm-Up 138 (page 144)

1. Mr., mister	5. Blvd., Boulevard	8. St., Saint
2. Sr., senior	6. Dec., December	9. Rd., Road
3. Jr., junior	7. Mon., Monday	10. Hwy., Highway
4. Dr., doctor		

11.–14. Check to make sure the students used each abbreviation in the sentence.

Warm-Up 139 (page 145)

1. Mon.	11. January, Jan.
2. Mar.	12. November, Nov.
3. Dec.	13. Wednesday, Wed.
4. Tue. or Tues.	14. February, Feb.
5. Apr.	15. October, Oct.
6. Fri.	16. Friday, Fri.
7. Thu. or Thurs.	17. Sunday, Sun.
8. May (no abbreviation for May)	18. September, Sept.
9. Aug.	19. December, Dec.
10. Saturday, Sat.	

Warm-Up 140 (page 146)

1. Arkansas, AR	12. DE
2. Florida, FL	13. OH
3. New York, NY	14. OR
4. West Virginia, WV	15. NE
5. South Carolina, SC	16. SD
6. Colorado, CO	17. NC
7. Idaho, ID	18. NJ
8. Massachusetts, MA	19. IN
9. North Dakota, ND	20. UT
10. Wyoming, WY	21. WI
11. CA	22. NM

Warm-Up 141 (page 147)
1. The bicycle has a basket, a horn, a seat, and a headlight.
2. Mike plays baseball, football, hockey, and basketball.
3. To plant a seed, dig a hole, put the seed in, cover the seed with soil, and water the seed.
4. Have you seen Millie, Molly, or Melly?
5. Do you want pumpkin, apple, or cherry pie?
6. The president, vice-president, secretary, and chairperson attended the fundraiser.
7. The elephant eats peanuts, hay, grass, and apples.
8. The baby cries, kicks, coos, chortles, and sighs.
9. Do you know how to play the piano, flute, organ, or trumpet?
10. Aunt Sally planted peach trees, apple trees, orange trees, and cherry trees.

Warm-Up 142 (page 148)
1. I don't know where the laundry chute is, <u>but</u> I do know where the trash chute is.
2. I like chocolate, <u>and</u> I like vanilla.
3. Margo was sick, <u>so</u> she missed the test.
4. My sister likes the attention, <u>yet</u> the rest of the family doesn't.
5. Do you want to take the stairs, <u>or</u> do you prefer to take the elevator?
6. Ava can have the boogie board, <u>or</u> she can have the sand toys.
7. Jordan built a fire, <u>and</u> he cooked the fish.
8. Lori does not have her cell phone, <u>nor</u> does she have a quarter to make a phone call.
9. The car broke down, <u>yet</u> everyone arrived on time.
10. Anna takes gymnastics, <u>so</u> she is very flexible.

Angelina wants to be a clothes designer, yet she does not sew very well. She has been taking sewing lessons for many years, but she still does not know how to sew on a button. Angelina hopes one day to learn how, but for now she just asks her mom to help her with sewing.

Warm-Up 143 (page 149)
1.–8. Check to make sure the students used a comma after the introductory clause.

Since Mom said that we could get a pet, we all went to the pet store. While we were looking at the rabbits, I saw the cutest puppy! He was so lively and had huge paws. When Mom saw the puppy, she agreed he was cute. Although we had planned on getting a rabbit, we ended up taking home a puppy!

Warm-Up 144 (page 150)
1.–6. Check to make sure the students have written the dates correctly.

Last month⌃ on July 15⌃ 2007⌃ my family and I went to visit our relatives in Cincinnati⌃ Ohio. Our relatives live in a two-story house at 3540 Sycamore Street. Our relatives⌃ Aunt Sue and Uncle Billy⌃ have five kids. The kids' names are Pat⌃ Larry⌃ Joe⌃ Darlene⌃ and Opal. Our cousins are in third grade⌃ fourth grade⌃ fifth grade⌃ sixth grade⌃ and seventh grade.

Warm-Up 145 (page 151)
1. Nancy's jacket
2. The Chihuahua's sweater
3. Susie's report card
4. Frankie's work
5. Wendy's computer
6.–10. Check to make sure the students have shown ownership in each sentence.

ANSWER KEY

Warm-Up 146 (page 152)

1. we're
2. aren't
3. he's
4. don't
5. it's
6. they'd
7. she'll
8. doesn't
9. won't
10. they're
11. I'm
12. you're

13. We're not going to be late for the train. or We aren't going to be late for the train.
14. He's getting another parking ticket!
15. Don't drive on the wrong side of the road.
16. I'm first in line.
17. They're moving to a new city.
18. This plan won't work.
19. This doesn't sound like a good idea to me.
20. She'll work hard at her new job.

Warm-Up 147 (page 153)

1. hoe
2. dirt
3. plants
4. stake
5. bush
6. broom

7.–12. Check to make sure the students have written an appropriate definition for each word.

Warm-Up 148 (page 154)

1. book
2. carpet
3. chair
4. clock
5. fireplace
6. mirror
7. picture
8. sofa
9. television
10. window

11.–14. Check to make sure the students have written appropriate sentences.

Warm-Up 149 (page 155)

1. blanket—chest
2. blanket
3. chest
4. brunch, calculator, checkers, breakfast, brick, cat, buy, cast, can, castle, bump

Warm-Up 150 (page 156)

barking–bracelet

bead	best
beak	bet
beard	better
bed	bland
bell	bled
belt	blend
bend	bottom

braid—bred

brain	break
brake	breath
bran	breathe
brand	

Warm-Up 151 (page 157)

do–egg

dug	ear	eel
each	east	
eagle	eat	

fan–ghost

fancy	field	fun
farm	fill	
fat	fruit	

Warm-Up 152 (page 158)

1. pup´ē, noun, a young dog
2. gäz´liŋ, noun, a young goose
3. duk´liŋ, noun, a young duck
4. kōlt, noun, a young male horse
5. kit´n, noun, a young cat
6. kaf, noun, a baby cow

7.–11. Check to make sure the students have added five more animals to the list.

Warm-Up 153 (page 159)

1.–9. Check to make sure the students have completed the assignment.

Warm-Up 154 (page 160)

Sample answers:

1. a flying mammal; a hard stick used to hit something with
2. something seen with the eye; a cutting tool
3. something to see with; a hole in the needle through which the thread goes through
4. a sticky piece used to hold items together; to record what was said
5. something that has music on it; an event that is written down or preserved for history

Warm-Up 155 (page 161)

Sample answers:

1. symbol used to represent sound for an instrument or a voice; a short letter
2. a scrape or injury to the body; to use scissors to change the shape or length of something
3. what one receives on a test; the year in school
4. a home for a farm animal; used to write with
5. to sway back and forth; a hard stone or pebble

Warm-Up 156 (page 162)

1. similar
2. familiar
3. knows
4. vacuum
5. raccoon
6. equipment
7. sandwich
8. grandma
9. cousin
10. suitcase
11. calendar
12. brother

Warm-Up 157 (page 163)

1. photograph
2. magazine
3. trophy
4. surprise
5. court
6. teacher
7. principal
8. army
9. cookie
10. sugar
11. California
12. motorcycle

Warm-Up 158 (page 164)

1. noun, adjective
2. noun, verb, adjective
3. noun, verb, adjective
4. noun, verb, adjective
5. noun, adverb, adjective
6. noun, adjective
7. noun
8. noun, adjective
9. noun
10. noun, verb

Warm-Up 159 (page 165)

1. bath, 1 syllable
2. Cor-nish, 2 syllables
3. daugh-ter, 2 syllables
4. e-piph-a-ny, 4 syllables
5. friend, 1 syllable
6. grand-moth-er, 3 syllables
7. hus-tle, 2 syllables
8. i-gua-na, 3 syllables
9. ju-ni-per, 3 syllables
10. key, 1 syllable
11. lis-ten-er, 3 syllables
12. mo-tion-less, 3 syllables